Drug Rehab

The 5 Things You *Absolutely* Need to Know Before You Go

Scott Pilara

Editing: Rick Benzel Creative Services, Los Angeles, CA.
www.rickbenzel.com

Cover and Book Design: fiverr.com/pro_ebookcovers

Book Formatting: fiverr.com/thebookformat

Published by The Power of Choice LLC
www.thepowerofchoice.com

First edition
ISBN: 978-0-9992979-0-2
eBook ISBN: 978-0-9992979-1-9

1. Twelve-step programs.
2. Addicts – Rehabilitation.
3. Substance abuse – Treatment.
4. Drug rehab – Heroin Addiction.
5. Non-twelve-step programs.

Table of Contents

Introduction 5

Part 1 – The Basic Info about Rehab........................... 8

Chapter 1 – Overview of the Rehab Industry and Its Fraudulent Ways 9

Chapter 2 – Understanding the Types of Treatment. 16

Part 2 - The Five Things to Know..............................31

#1 – There is No Correlation Between Program Cost and Effectiveness.. 32

#2 – Small Facilities May Be Better Than Big 39

#3 – Medications Are Not the Complete Answer 78

#4 - You Don't Need to Travel Across Country for Rehab 102

#5 - Effective Treatment is Not What You May Think It Is..111

Introduction

Addiction and mental health disorders in America are at epidemic levels. An estimated 43.6 million Americans over the age of 18 suffer from mental illness and 21.5 million suffer from a substance abuse disorder. Only 10% per year receive the assistance they need to get help.[1]

The substance abuse and mental health treatment industry is, nevertheless, massive. Over 14,000 different facilities in the United States treat a myriad of substance abuse and mental health concerns. Researching where one should go to receive help can be a daunting task. Just the choice of treatments itself can be confusing: dual diagnosis, MAT (medication-assisted treatment), abstinence-based, evidence-based, harm reduction, 12-step, non-12-step, holistic, and others. What do all these mean and what are their differences? Which one is right for you or your loved one?

---

[1] Sarra L. Hedden et al, "Behavioral Health Trends in the United States: Results from the 2014 National Survey on Drug Use and Health," *SAMHSA*, September 2015, https://www.samhsa.gov/data/sites/default/files/NSDUH-FRR1-2014/NSDUH-FRR1-2014.pdf

Answering your questions is what this book is for. I will explain these concepts in detail and provide you with five vital things you need to know before you or your loved one go into a rehab facility. I am in a unique position to share information that up until now has never been made available to the public, as I have more than ten years of in-depth experience in the substance abuse treatment industry.

In 2008, I founded The Power of Choice™ (www.thepowerofchoice.com), the first concierge substance abuse treatment service in the United States. I have worked at the most exclusive residential treatment center in the US as a tech, a life coach, and as a sober companion. I later went on to develop a concierge detox program catering to some of the wealthiest and most successful executives in America (Yes, professionally successful people can suffer from addiction). I have also been the director of operations for a sub-acute residential detox facility, which primarily detoxed opioid addicts brought in off the streets. At one time, I also owned the most exclusive sober living facility in the country located in Malibu, California. I have seen just about everything to see in the industry both good and bad.

My intention in writing this book is not to give specific recommendations about which treatment center to select. Each person's needs and background to addiction are unique. My goal is also not to dissuade anyone from seeking help for a substance abuse or mental health concern at a hospital or residential facility. Rather, I am motivated to help you avoid the most common pitfalls I have seen too many people fall into while navigating these confusing choices. No one should fall victim to the misinformation commonly presented to those searching for help in this difficult time in their lives.

The majority of the book is devoted to 5 serious misconceptions, if not intentional deceptions, that treatment industry insiders commonly use to mislead the public, intentionally misrepresenting the effectiveness of their programs solely for their own profit. This is not an exhaustive list, but after 10 years of working in the industry, I have learned that these 5 issues play a crucial role in the success or failure of treatment. They are significant considerations to take into account when researching which treatment center is best for you or your loved one.

I am under no illusion that exposing this information will win me any popularity contests in the treatment industry. In fact, I can guarantee that what I will share is information treatment center owners definitely do not want an unsuspecting public to know about. These are the "tricks of the trade" that owners use to exploit addicts, their loved ones, and the insurance benefits that are designed to help addicts heal.

Part 1 – The Basic Info about Rehab

Chapter 1 – Overview of the Rehab Industry and Its Fraudulent Ways

I am frequently asked questions like: "Can you recommend a treatment center?" and "Where should I send my son, daughter, spouse, or friend?" After working in the industry for a decade as a support staff technician, life coach, sober companion, director of operations, and as an owner, I am quick to tell people that they must first look within themselves to figure out what they would like to achieve by entering rehab. Ask questions like:

- What the underlying reasons are that drive me to use drugs and/or alcohol as a coping mechanism?
- Do I possess the humility to accept the fact that I do not know why I continue to make the same self-sabotaging decisions over and over again?
- Am I willing to listen to someone who may be able to share their wisdom with me even though it may be something that I do not want to hear?
- Do I already know the reasons as to why I repeatedly engage in self-destructive behavior, or maybe I just don't care what those reasons

are, and I simply want to heal the physical damage caused by my addiction?

- Am I willing to put in the hard work to create a sober life once I leave treatment?

- What are my plans once I leave treatment? Do I plan on starting over somewhere else or do I plan on returning home and carrying on with my existing life?

Perhaps you don't have an answer to these questions yet, but you simply need to figure out a place to go dry out. Fair enough. But if you want to end the vicious cycle of addiction you will need to figure out the answers to these questions at some point.

What I can tell you is that not all treatment centers are the same, but to the layperson who has never been through treatment before, figuring out where to go can be an overwhelming experience.

In fairness of full disclosure, I am by no means a fan of the residential treatment industry. In fact, I am writing another book on the rehab industry as a whole, an exposé if you will that dives deeper into the abuses, misdeeds and ineffectiveness of residential treatment. Within the pages of that book, I will highlight some of the most egregious transgressions that occur within residential treatment centers across the country on a daily basis, as well as why treatment outcomes historically are so poor and why they will continue to worsen under the current treatment paradigm.

Unfortunately, people will still seek out help for their mental health or substance abuse concerns at residential facilities. They have been conditioned to believe that is what they should do to heal from their addictions. They also think that, as of the writing of this book, health insurance pays for it so why not give it a try. Besides, it works for some people, so why can't you or your loved one be one of the fortunate souls who figures it out in rehab.

My goal here is to help you sift through the huge marketing noise in this industry. In actuality, only between 5% to 10% of admitted patients to 12-step treatment programs stay abstinent following treatment,[2] and only a few treatment centers have programs that in my view are worthy of the expense. My objective is to provide you with information that will assist you to make an informed decision as to where you or your loved one or friend should go to seek treatment. I will especially educate you on what questions you should be asking when you are speaking to rehab "salesmen," by which I mean intake and admissions coordinators.

Salesmen. That's right! Rehab is a business, a big business. By some estimates, the industry exceeds $35

---

[2] Lance Dodes, MD, Zachary Dodes, *The Sober Truth* (Boston: Beacon Press), 1-2.

billion a year in revenue[3], with some of the larger facilities earning hundreds of millions of dollars annually. When you call the 800 number on the rehab website, you will be speaking with a salesman, one who in most cases is financially incentivized to sell you on their program.

No different from a car salesman who has you on their lot, rehab salesmen understand that their best opportunity to close you on their program is while you are on the phone with them. Once you hang up, they know there are thousands of other facilities to choose from.

It is not uncommon for intake and admissions coordinators (salesmen) to make misleading statements and false promises in an attempt to get you to commit to their facility. You will hear statements like: "We offer X amount of hours of clinical programming each week," "We offer more one-to-one therapy than any other facility in the country," "We only use evidence-based therapies," "We are a holistic program," or "We have the finest team of therapists anywhere." Worst are the promises: "Our treatment outcomes are some of the highest in the country," and the grand finale: "We can cure addiction."

What is most alarming is that no government

---

[3] Dan Munro, "Inside the $35 Billion Treatment Industry," *Forbes,* April 27, 2015, https://www.forbes.com/sites/danmunro/2015/04/27/inside-the-35-billion-addiction-treatment-industry/ - 61e818a917dc

agencies or regulatory bodies hold the industry accountable. No performance standards are in place to force treatment centers to prove that the clinical programming they offer actually works, or that what they advertise in the way of services and amenities is even factual. They can write anything on their website, and the salesperson can say pretty much whatever lures you in. You only learn the truth after you have already committed and are under their care. That is a scary proposition, especially if you are considering admitting into a treatment center out of your state or on the other side of the country.

For a time, I worked as the director of operations of a sub-acute detox facility in Woodland Hills, California that advertised clinical therapeutic programming such as art and music therapy (not true). The owners marketed themselves as an abstinence-based program located in beautiful, sunny Malibu (also not true). Most of the clients we received came from locations out of state, mainly Kentucky and Ohio, so it was more marketable to position themselves as a Malibu-based facility that was within close proximity to the beach when in reality it was located in the heart of San Fernando Valley, some 20 miles from the nearest beach.

From a business perspective, this made perfect sense, albeit a highly unethical one, because by the time clients arrived, they were already across the United States and were either too high or too dope sick to question where they had arrived. It was only after their fog started to wear off a few days later that they would ask where the beach was. I can also confirm that almost every client was discharged on some kind of medication they were put on while under our care, and that there was absolutely no meaningful clinical programming of any kind offered, let alone art or music therapy. I wish I could say that this is a rare occurrence in the industry, and that most treatment centers run effective and ethical programs, but that is rarely the case.

In 2008, the United States government interjected itself into the treatment industry when Congress passed The Mental Health Parity and Addiction Equity Act, which mandated that health insurers could not restrict or deny benefits for mental health or addiction treatment. Initially, this piece of legislation only applied to group health plans and health insurance issuers until the act was amended with the passing of the Affordable Care Act (Obamacare) and the Health Care and Education Reconciliation Act in 2010.

Today, I would speculate that more than 95% of the 2 million people who seek treatment do so through a health insurance plan. The government demonstrated a sincere willingness to provide increased access to treatment, but they dropped the ball when they stopped short of holding the treatment industry accountable to minimum performance standards. I am not usually one to pound the table for increased government regulations, but there needs to be some form of Congressional oversight on this industry, or a regulatory body that holds industry participants' feet to the fire. Government needs to mandate treatment centers to prove that their treatment actually works, and that the services, amenities, and location claimed in their marketing are indeed factual. Until this paradigm shifts, we will continue to be stuck with our current ineffective system of treatment that exploits a growing addict population. Meanwhile everyone who pays for health insurance will continue to shoulder the real financial burden as our health insurance premiums continue to skyrocket.

Chapter 2 – Understanding the Types of Treatment

B efore diving into the 5 factors to watch out for, it is useful to have an understanding of the most common forms of detox and rehabilitation treatment available and in use today. Most treatment centers subscribe to a specific methodology or at least a philosophical foundation that their clinical program is built upon.

I cannot stress enough how imperative it is that you possess a clear understanding of the different treatment options currently available within the United States. Treatment can be administered in any number of ways and combinations. The key is to figure out what resonates most with you, and then fully commit to your program like it's a full-time job, which it should be, at least initially.

I believe there are far more progressive and effective treatment options offered outside of the United States, but the focus of the book is geared towards those within the U.S. Since you are most likely using your health insurance to pay for a majority of your program, I limit my discussion to the treatments used in this country.

Dual diagnosis

Dual Diagnosis treatment facilities address both substance abuse disorder(s) concurrently with presenting psychiatric disorder(s), that is, co-occurring mood and/or behavioral disorders. Some examples of psychiatric disorders include depression, bipolar disorder, schizophrenia, personality disorder, anxiety disorder, sex addiction, eating disorders, compulsive gambling, technology addiction, and so on. In many cases, a psychiatric condition will develop first, and then, out of a need to cope with the discomfort of the condition, the person will turn to drugs, alcohol, or process addictions to self-soothe.

Up through the mid-1990's, treatment facilities would typically treat substance abuse disorders separately from psychiatric disorders, otherwise known as sequential treatment. This type of treatment would typically address the substance abuse disorder first, prior to the presenting psychiatric disorder. Research studies examining the efficacy of sequential treatment versus dual diagnosis treatment reported higher relapse rates among the former. As a result, sequential treatment has been phased out in favor of dual diagnosis treatment.

Most residential treatment centers today offer dual diagnosis treatment for co-occurring disorders. Some make the claim that treating co-occurring disorders is different than dual diagnosis treatment in that dual diagnosis treatment programs merely manage mental health symptoms through the use of medication, while co-occurring disorder programs work to address the underlying issues that drive substance abuse and presenting mental health disorder(s) through therapy. In my view, this is just semantics used to mislead. Unless the program is abstinence-based and does not use medication, any program that uses medication does so to manage symptoms. That is what western addiction medicine is, symptom management. Therapy, whether it be integrative, talk therapy, or experiential, is facilitated with the intention to address the underlying psychological drivers of addiction and/or mental health challenges.

MAT (Medication-Assisted Treatment)

Medication-assisted treatment is exactly what it sounds like. Treatment centers use medications in conjunction with behavioral therapy to address substance abuse and psychiatric disorders. While medications for substance abuse disorders have been used within treatment settings for quite some time, this approach has gained considerably more traction as the opioid crisis has aggressively swept across America. As part of the $31.1 billion National Drug Control Budget for 2017, President Obama earmarked $1 billion to fund expanded access to treatment services for those who are seeking to overcome opioid abuse disorder.

The medications commonly used to manage the symptoms of opioid abuse disorder are Buprenorphine, Naltrexone, and Methadone, and they are commonly prescribed in conjunction with a myriad of other medications designed to manage symptoms of withdrawal, as well as any presenting psychiatric disorder(s). There are positives and negatives associated with using medication to combat addiction, which I will speak to in greater detail in later chapters.

Abstinence Based

The core focus of this treatment is total abstinence from all drug use, including pharmaceutical medications commonly used as narcotic substitutes in treating opioid addiction. There are many 12-step proponents who preach that if a person is attending 12-step meetings and they are on medication, even if it's for a legitimate psychiatric condition like bipolar disorder, then they are not truly sober. This position walks a slippery slope as it is nothing more than an opinion, and by no means scientifically true. Abstinence-based treatment tends to be the common approach to treating alcohol, cocaine, and methamphetamine abuse disorders, and far less common for treating opioid addiction.

Evidence-Based Therapy (EBT)

Evidence-based therapy (EBT), or evidence based practice (EBP) is a term you will commonly see on most every treatment center's website today. What evidence-based therapy refers to are therapeutic techniques and approaches whose efficacy is backed or supported by scientific evidence. The most common types of evidence-based therapy facilitated in treatment centers are Cognitive Behavioral Therapy (CBT), Dialectical Behavioral Therapy (DBT), Rational Emotive Behavioral Therapy (REBT), and Motivation Interviewing (MI), but there are several other forms such as Acceptance and Commitment Therapy (ACT), Mindfulness-Based Stress Reduction (MBSR), Mindfulness-Based Cognitive Therapy (MBCT), Compassion-Focused Therapy (CFT), and Imago Relationship Therapy.

There are a number of critiques of EBT. One is that its foundation is rooted in the movement of the early 90's towards the managed-care model of medicine. In that, the pharmaceutical and health insurance industries created a health care system that rewards over-prescribing of prescription drugs and psychotropic medications, tools to manage the underlying symptoms of poor physical and mental health, without truly addressing the root cause of illness.

With the recent requirement that health insurers

provide benefits to cover substance abuse and mental health treatment, the residential treatment industry has effectively joined this trend of managed care medicine. Health insurance companies dictate which forms of treatment qualify for reimbursement, regardless if they work or not, and every decision made in residential treatment revolves around reimbursement of a fee-for-service. But addiction is a symptom of unaddressed psychological and physiological dis-ease rooted within one's Soul, and no form of pharmaceutical medication will transmute it.

A second critique of EBT is that the definition of "evidence" is inconclusive, and the means and methods used to measure the efficacy and/or effectiveness of evidence based therapies remains subjective. A third critique of EBT is that it neglects to consider the skill level of the clinicians facilitating the therapy. Not all therapists are equally effective, and most of the nation's most gifted therapists do not even work in residential treatment but rather maintain their own private practices. In the end, the quality and types of therapy in most residential treatment facilities are subpar to what is available in private practice offerings.

Harm Reduction

Harm reduction is a relatively new concept in the world of substance abuse treatment in that it does not subscribe to the ideology of total abstinence. Rather, harm reduction accepts that both licit and illicit drug use is a facet of life in our society. It therefore takes the position that therapy can be effective if it works to minimize the harmful effects of using drugs, without minimizing or ignoring their dangers. This approach tends to be viewed as more empowering than other approaches of working with addictions in that it recognizes that each person's path to addiction is specific to his or her own biological, psychological, and social interactions with their drug(s) of choice. It allows for clients to set and prioritize their own treatment goals. The approach does not subscribe to using demeaning labels like "addict" or "alcoholic" when referring to program participants, nor does it force participants to identify with having a disease. Harm reduction strategies are typically used in conjunction with evidence-based therapeutic interventions in treatment settings. For example, there are some residential treatment programs using cannabis both for opioid detox, and as a harm reduction tool to encourage addicts to switch to a physiologically safer substance.

12-Step

There are 35 or so different types of 12-step meetings that address everything from alcohol abuse to food, sex or gambling addiction to addiction to specific drugs such as cocaine, methamphetamine, or heroin.

The foundation of all 12-step groups is rooted in AA (Alcoholics Anonymous), created by Bill Wilson and Dr. Bob Smith in the 1930's. Bill Wilson was a compulsive drinker who had been hospitalized on four different occasions due to his alcohol problem. It is said that it was during his fourth hospital stay, he experienced a spiritual awakening, and it was through that experience he was prompted to create AA.

AA and Narcotics Anonymous (NA) are two of the oldest forms of treatment available, but statistically they are not any more or less effective than 12-step residential rehab programs, with success rates hovering somewhere between 5-10%.[4] One of the primary reasons why AA and NA are so prevalent as methods of treatment within our society is because our legal system often mandates that addicts attend meetings for alcohol and/or drug offenders. A second reason is that it is free. Up until the Mental Health Parity and Addiction Equity of 2008, most treatment facilities were cost prohibitive for a large segment of the population, while attending 12-step meetings does not cost participants a dime. Third, many treatment programs use outside 12-step meetings as part of their clinical programming because it also does not cost them anything, while it fills up time on the clinical schedule. I have even heard stories of facilities trying

4 Lance Dodes, MD, Zachary Dodes, *The Sober Truth* (Boston: Beacon Press), 1-2.

to bill their patient's health insurance for outside 12-step meetings, as if it were a group therapy session.

There are numerous shortcomings with the 12-step approach. First, it claims that addiction is a disease but nowhere in the steps does it address how to heal the underlying physiological drivers of addiction. Two, the philosophy and system is dogmatic, backward looking, and makes no attempt to affirm positive character traits. Step 1 starts as a negative affirmation (affirming powerlessness), and from that step, the remaining ones do not affirm an individuals' power of free will, putting the responsibility of facilitating change onto one's God. For those who are not religious or spiritual, the references to God can be offensive and so the strategy does not work for some people. Third, it is not uncommon for the newly sober to "take each other out," so if you are feeling like you want a great place to meet people who share your drug of choice, go to a 12-step meeting. Fourth, females and newcomers to 12-step meetings who have less than a year of abstinence are routinely preyed upon sexually by what are referred to as 13th-steppers, AA and NA old timers who target newcomers for their own sexual gratification. Bill Wilson, the founder of AA and the 12-step movement was a notorious philanderer. The term 13th-stepper was conceived as a product of his well-documented escapades of targeting young women new to 12-step meetings, and sleeping with them. Fifth, there is an embedded shaming component if an individual relapses because they "lose their sobriety days," a potentially dangerous notion to self-esteem.

In my experience of working in treatment, a tremendous amount of learning about one's motives to use drugs or alcohol can be gained during periods of relapse. One can discover deeper aspects of the Self, what our triggers are, and what we need to avoid in order to create a safe and healthy environment for ourselves moving forward. I say this not as a justification for relapse because relapse can be life threatening and very dangerous, but there is wisdom to be gained through all of our life's trials and tribulations, including relapse.

Ultimately, AA, NA, and other 12-step meetings and groups are not effective forms of treatment; if anything, they are merely forms of fellowship. I would advise against choosing a treatment facility that bases its clinical program around a 12-step methodology, as they are statistically proven to be ineffective.

Non-12-Step

Non-12-step approaches are gaining in popularity for some of the aforementioned reasons I mentioned above. Some examples of non-12-step forms of fellowship are Women for Sobriety, Secular Organizations for Sobriety (SOS), LifeRing, Secular Recovery, Celebrate Recovery, the Life Process Program, Moderation Management, SMART Recovery and others. Non-12-step programs tend to be less dogmatic in their approach to transmuting the "addicted state." A number of these programs use "evidence-based" therapeutic approaches, and tend to avoid labels like addict and alcoholic. As scientific evidence on addiction has evolved, so too have the foundational concepts of many of these approaches, and they all tend to support the concept that the power of an individual's free will is necessary to create lasting change.

I cannot stress enough how important and powerful recognizing and cultivating the concept of free will is for those looking to overcome addiction. People become sober because they choose to, and for no other reason. Each day, a new choice must be made as to whether or not we stay sober, or if we choose to use, it is our choice. Addiction treatment—outside of the medical/physiological component—is merely nothing more than providing tools to assist an individual to have the ability to make healthy, self-supportive choices.

When you are looking at treatment facilities that follow this addiction recovery fellowship, look to see what tools you or your loved one will be provided with, educate yourself on what those tools are and how they work, and ask yourself if the tools resonate with you.

Integrative Treatment (Holistic)

Integrative treatment addresses the body (physical), mind (mental and emotional), and spirit as one interconnected entity. Teaching the concept of mindfulness tends to be an overarching theme among holistic rehabs/integrative treatment approaches. The idea is to stay in the present moment, and to accept the current state of ones' mental, emotional, physical and spiritual wellbeing. Examples of some of the tools used to teach this concept are yoga, tai chi, qi gong, energy medicine, body work, acupuncture, meditation, conscious eating, nutritional counseling, bio- and neuro-feedback, physical fitness, spiritual counseling, art and music therapy. In conjunction with these modalities, it is not uncommon for a treatment facility to incorporate either 12-step or non-12-step methods of treatment/fellowship, as well as "evidence-based" methods of talk therapy. Imbalances, deficiencies and pathologies can be addressed using Western and/or Eastern medicine in conjunction with the aforementioned therapies and healing arts. Unfortunately, the most effective forms of holistic addiction medicine, in my view, are available outside of the United States. The reasons why fall outside the scope of this book, but I do address the cause of this fact in my upcoming book.

In the end, the choice of treatment methods has to be yours, because it has to work for you. The goal of sobriety is not simply to string a bunch of days of abstinence together. Rather, it is to change and uplift one's consciousness to the point where drugs and/or alcohol are no longer part of your everyday awareness. That is real sobriety. In the event of a relapse, you don't start over. You take what you have learned about yourself, what you need to do to be mentally, emotionally, physically, and spiritually healthy, and you implement that information into your life to move forward. Starting over again mentally at Day 1 implies loss, which is a dangerous and outdated concept that serves no one's highest and best interests. This is especially true for those who are trying to put an already fragile life back together again, and for those who need continuous unconditional support without feeling shamed or judged.

The "customized treatment" ploy

The last point I need to make in this chapter is about the misnomer that many facilities utilize when they advertise "customized treatment programs." Let's get clear as to what that really means.

As mentioned in the previous chapter, I estimate that at least 95% of all individuals who seek treatment do it through a health insurance plan. One of the many stipulations that health insurance companies require of treatment centers to capture insurance reimbursement is that each patient must receive a clinical program that addresses their specific needs. However, all residential treatment programs utilize a "one-size-fits-all" approach to treating their clients, even the most expensive ones in the country. Some programs offer more individual therapy than group therapy, but even within those facilities, everyone receives the same type of clinical programming— unless they want to pay even more. So how do the treatment facilities go about claiming they have customized treatment programs when every client under their roof receives the exact same treatment? Simple.

What it boils down to is making sure the clinical notes the therapists are required to submit after each group or individual session speak to the specific issues that each individual client is facing. In the most basic terms, physicians, therapists, and all other documenting clinicians must submit client-specific treatment notes so as to not simply "copy and paste" the same notes from one client to the next (which actually does happen anyway). Technically, all treatment centers that bill insurance benefits are thus providing "individualized" treatment programs, but nothing about it is truly an individualized form of treatment. I have seen countless treatment facilities use this claim as one of the marketing ploys designed to entice prospective clients when it is purely a misrepresentation of their clinical programming. The saddest part is that this ploy comes at the expense of addicts who desperately need individualized treatment programming.

Part 2 - The Five Things to Know

#1 – There is No Correlation Between Program Cost and Effectiveness

Program cost is not a driver of program efficacy. In fact, the most expensive residential treatment centers in the country cannot prove their programs are any more effective than if you were to simply start attending free 12-step meetings in your local church basement. What you will receive at the expensive facilities are ocean views (if you're in Southern California), and nicer amenities (higher thread counts, turn down service, and possibly a swimming pool and/or tennis court on the property). The costliest residential treatment programs in the country claim to offer more individual therapy, as opposed to group therapy, but even they cannot prove that their clinical programming actually works with greater success, or is in any way a contributing factor in a person's ability to achieve sobriety upon discharge.

Program cost also does not translate to a higher level of patient care. Running a residential treatment facility is very expensive, and the overhead expenditures combined with the outsized salaries the owners pay themselves (as compared to what the hands-on clinicians actually make) absorb a significant portion of revenues. Owners have a tendency to cut costs whenever possible, and unfortunately those cuts usually revolve around the quality of patient care. In fact, with the introduction of insurance benefits covering treatment, the mission has become to maximize insurance reimbursement while simultaneously minimizing costs.

Here is an example of a cost-cutting strategy. In 2008, I was working as a life coach at one of Malibu's $60,000+/per month rehab facilities when it began to accept insurance benefits. The owners quickly saw that the amount they received from the insurance companies was far less than what they were billing. This is par for the course in the insurance field, which pays only an "allowed" amount despite what a medical facility might bill. (It's the difference between the billed amount versus how much the insurer decides they will allow for each procedure.) Believing they were losing money, the owners made the decision to start "trimming the fat" in an effort to maintain their former high profit margins. The "fat" turned out to be the salaries of the most qualified and gifted senior clinicians on staff. A mass exodus then occurred, as most of the therapists left, many of whom had over 20 years of clinical experience and had been working at the facility for years. In their place, the owners hired either newly licensed therapists who had just recently completed the clinical hours required to sit for licensure, or therapists who only had a few years of

33

unsupervised clinical experience. To say that the quality of care diminished would be an understatement. Did the owners lower the cost of the program due to the lower quality of care that they were offering? Of course not; in fact they raised it by another $15,000 a month, and one of the owners purchased a new Porsche Turbo.

Another example -- same principle but in a different context. An acupuncturist colleague of mine, with whom I have worked on several private client cases, was approached by an exclusive residential treatment facility to work for them. They wanted her to treat up to 12 clients at a time in a group acupuncture setting, and they were offering to pay her $75 per hour (not even half of her normal hourly rate). If this were a treatment center on the lower end of the price scale, I would not be shocked. But at a treatment center that costs north of $70,000 a month, one should expect to receive, at the least, several 50-minute private sessions per month with an acupuncturist.

By offering group acupuncture, rather than individual acupuncture, the facility can bill each of the 12 patients' insurance for a 1-hour session (12 hours in total), while only paying the clinician for one hour of work. This system of treatment satisfies the clinical programming requirements insurance companies impose on treatment centers to be eligible to receive reimbursement. Insurance companies mandate a minimum standard of clinical care be maintained if the facility is to receive reimbursement, and part of that minimum standard are the number of hours of eligible treatment (psychotherapy, chemical dependency counseling, hypnotherapy, acupuncture, etc.) that a patient receives each day. Fitting 12 clients into a group acupuncture session meets both requirements (type of reimbursable treatment and time). Plus, the treatment center can still advertise, misleadingly, that they offer acupuncture as a form of treatment without disclosing that it is group acupuncture.

From a clinical treatment standpoint, this ruse is especially harmful to the person as well because the group acupuncture treatment format simply manages the physical symptoms of addiction and withdrawal, rather than healing the underlying physiological drivers of the addicted state, which is what an individual hour-long individual acupuncture session would be intending to do.

If you do the math, this deception is outrageous. If the facility bills each patient's health insurance $400 for the acupuncture session, times 12 clients receiving treatment, it equals $4800 in billings for a one-hour session, for which the facility only pays the acupuncturist $75. Realistically, they will probably collect about half, or maybe a little bit more than half of this amount from the insurance companies because they have a JCAHO accreditation (more accreditations in the next chapter), but you are still looking at $2325 in revenue. If you were to give each client their own hour, which they should be entitled to for $70,000 month, it would cost the facility $900 to pay the acupuncturist versus only $75. You can see why treatment centers offer as much group therapy/treatment as possible while limiting the one-to-one, which is far more beneficial. When my colleague told me about the offer she received, and what the job entailed, I wasn't surprised by the owners' lack of ethical considerations for his clients. This facility has a reputation for kicking their clients out with less than 24 hours' notice when their insurance benefits run out and the client cannot come up with the cash to pay for the remainder of their treatment.

This greed is normal in the industry, where the quality of client care is continually sacrificed in the name of profitability. Unfortunately, it's the unsuspecting public who put their lives and trust into these programs, thinking that for the outrageous sums of money some of these facilities charge, they will receive the highest quality care possible. This is rarely the case.

The key takeaway here is that the cost of a treatment program has no relation to how effective it will be for you. You might think that the quality of care improves in direct relation to price, but there is no guarantee of this. The expensive facilities charge a lot of money and offer nicer amenities, gourmet food (which is not necessarily healthy), better outings, and sometimes more one-to-one treatment, but it does not mean that the outcome will be any better than a low-priced facility.

If you can afford high end treatment, make sure you get a clear understanding of what you are paying for. Verify it by touring the facility for yourself if you can. Meet with the owners, talk to the staff, and, if possible, speak with current clients to get an unfiltered opinion as to the quality of their treatment and care. Ask the staff members how long they have worked there, what the turnover is (it's extremely high within the industry), and if they enjoy working there (what they like and not like). If you do not feel good about the owners, clinicians, or support staff members, I can guarantee you will not like the facility because they all very much adhere to a "top down" structure. Like most businesses, the culture of each facility begins with its owner(s) and trickles down through the staff.

Find out how many actual one-to-one treatment hours you will receive each week and with whom they will be facilitated, what forms of one-to-one treatment you will receive, how many hours and what type of group therapy you will receive, who will be on your clinical team, how much experience they have (years working in the substance abuse field), and whether you can make changes to your treatment plan if you find that you resonate with certain therapies more than others. Ask also if you will be charged extra for any changes. Most importantly, ask if they can provide you with proof that shows unequivocally that their treatment program/concept works—specifically, how many or what percentage of their clients stay sober for at least one year upon leaving.

If you like what you hear, ask them to put their answers to your questions in writing. The goal is to hold them accountable that you will receive everything they claim to provide. If they say they cannot do that, e.g., "writing it down for you is not something we do," take it as a sign you are being sold a bill of goods. Start looking for another treatment option elsewhere that is willing to hold themselves accountable for their services and the amenities they advertise.

#2 – Small Facilities May Be Better Than Big

The substance abuse treatment industry is massive and growing. There are currently over 14,000 licensed addiction and mental health treatment facilities in the United States. The annual revenues for the industry are estimated to be around $35 billion a year, trending towards $42 billion a year by 2020.[5] That figure is higher than Walmart's operating cash flow in 2016, and they are the largest retailer in the world.

A combination of a factors has spurred the industry's growth since 2008. First, the health insurance industry and Medicaid were mandated by law to provide benefits to policy holders for treating substance abuse disorders. Secondly, America has become infested with an opioid epidemic, due to the pharmaceutical industry, not street drugs, and alcoholism now effects 1 out of every 8 adults in

---

[5] Teri Sforza, "Addiction Treatment: The New Gold Rush. 'It's almost chic'," *The Orange County Register*, June 16, 2017, http://www.ocregister.com/2017/06/16/addiction-treatment-the-new-gold-rush-its-almost-chic/

America.[6]

Here is the alarming factoid about that: in 2015, out of the roughly 2.6 million people reported to have an opioid addiction, only .6 million had a substance abuse disorder involving heroin, while 2 million were addicted to pharmaceutical opioids.[7] This means roughly 77% of all people hooked on opioids are addicted to painkillers, while the remaining 23% are addicted to heroin (addicts who more than likely got started on prescription painkillers). It is not uncommon for prescription opioid addicts to eventually turn to heroin because it is cheaper and easier to get. Conversely, in areas of the country where heroin is more difficult to come by, addicts will turn to prescription opioids to "keep themselves well." What we typically hear via the media is that America has a heroin problem, when the truth of the matter is that American has a prescription opioid problem that gives birth to heroin addiction. What we don't hear as much about is the 88,000 people who die a year due to alcohol related illness and events, and nearly 30

---

6 Christopher Ingraham, "One in Eight America Adults is an Alcoholic, study says," *The Washington Post*, August 11, 2017, https://www.washingtonpost.com/news/wonk/wp/2017/08/11/study-one-in-eight-american-adults-are-alcoholics/?utm_term=.197da08c90cc&wpisrc=nl_rainbow&wpmm=1
7 Opioid Addiction 2016 Facts & Figures," *American Society of Addiction* Medicine, https://www.asam.org/docs/default-source/advocacy/opioid-addiction-disease-facts-figures.pdf

million Americans suffer from alcohol addiction.[8]

This rapid surge of new cases of addiction, coupled with required insurance dollars to pay for treatment has caused the addiction treatment world to explode. With money to be made, Wall Street has now entered the mix, with large corporations investing hundreds of millions of dollars to acquire and create additional treatment beds. With little federal and state oversight, the world of addiction treatment has become almost as unruly as the Wild West of the late 1800s.

The big players in the industry are swallowing up the little fish by buying them out. Upper echelon "niche" facilities compete against each other over who can offer the nicest amenities and the best ocean view. Facilities that cater to the more marginalized segments of our population offer inducements for free sober living if patients attend intensive outpatient sessions (IOP) in order to continue to collect Medicaid and insurance reimbursement, and cash kickbacks for committing to treatment are commonplace (and illegal). Insurance fraud and billing for unnecessary medical tests is widespread, the costs of which are passed onto all health insurance policy holders in the form of substantial increases to our monthly premiums.

---

[8] German Lopez, "It's not just opioid addiction. Alcoholism may be on the rise too," *Vox*, August 10, 2017, https://www.vox.com/policy-and-politics/2017/8/10/16124938/study-alcoholism-addiction-epidemic

Another phenomenon, which unfortunately is more prevalent than you might think, is that patients die in treatment. In California alone, one patient dies on average about every two weeks in a licensed residential treatment facility.[9] This is an abhorrent statistic. What is equally unacceptable is the greed driving the growth of the industry. It is fair to say most patient deaths are related to the facility's owner's addiction to money and profit. I will speak more to this point later on in the chapter.

Wall Street corporations have recognized the growth opportunity in addiction treatment and they are going all in. Acadia Healthcare, a publicly-traded company that operates a chain of addiction and mental health facilities, has seen their revenues increase from $413.8 million in 2012 to $2.85 billion in 2016, an increase of 700%. American Addiction Centers, another publicly-traded company specializing in addiction treatment has witnessed their revenues rise from $28.3 million in 2011 to $279.8 million in 2016. That's an increase of almost 1000% over a 5-year period. Deerfield Management, a private equity firm based out of New York, agreed to invest $231.5 million in Recovery Centers of America to create 1,200 additional treatment beds by the end of 2017. These are huge

---

9 Teri Sforza et al, "How some Southern California drug rehab centers exploit addiction," *The Orange County Register*, May 21, 2017, http://www.ocregister.com/2017/05/21/how-some-southern-california-drug-rehab-centers-exploit-addiction/

numbers!!!

So what are the differences between big treatment facilities—those that are publicly-traded or have the financial backing of private equity firms versus the smaller "mom and pop" 6-to-12 bed facilities? Effectively, the answer is that it depends. It depends on the motivations of the owner or ownership group who operate them. Publicly-traded companies and companies backed by private equity firms or hedge funds are solely motivated by profit. In fact, as a further point of consideration, be wary of treatment centers and addiction call centers that advertise on television; that is a tip-off that they are only in it for the money.

Even non-profit treatment centers are motivated by money. With an annual operating budget of around $180 million, Hazeldon Betty Ford is the largest and most well-known non-profit treatment facility in the county. One would be naïve to think that non-profit treatment facilities are not concerned with their bottom line, as they too adjust their clinical programming in ways to adhere to the *minimum* standard of clinical care mandated by the health insurance industry as a way to minimize their operating costs.

What you will find at many of the larger hospital-like facilities are treatment programs designed to conform to a minimum standard of acceptable, and thus reimbursable, care. One question to ask when speaking with an intake salesman is "What is the current census (head count) at the facility, and what is the maximum number of clients you accept at one time?" One of the big differences between treatment on the East Coast versus treatment on the West Coast is there are more hospital-like treatment environments on the East Coast. These are institutional facilities that can have as many as a few hundred patients at a time under one roof. On the West Coast, there are far more of the smaller residential treatment facilities which generally house a maximum of six patients at a time under one roof (big difference!).

Hospital-based treatment typically translates into a person receiving mostly group therapy with maybe, at best, one to two individual therapy sessions a week with either a chemical dependency counselor or a therapist. There is a high client-to-therapeutic staff ratio, underqualified low-paid and overworked staff, poor food quality with low nutritional value (non-organic GMO foods), and an overall low quality of care.

You might be asking why is it important to eat high nutritional value organic foods? It's because your brain is powered by your blood, and your blood is comprised of what you eat, and what you put in and on your body. If you are trying to heal and repair your brain, high-quality, nutrient-rich organic food is vital. So be sure to ask about the food, and have them send you a sample menu before you commit.

Unfortunately, we are now seeing the profit-maximizing business model being adopted at many smaller facilities as well. The cost of running a treatment facility is high. The smaller 6-bed residential facilities do not have the economies of scale to spread the cost over as many "heads." A way for them to cut costs (and this goes for the larger facilities as well) is on whom they hire. For support staff (called techs), undereducated, poorly skilled, and former patients newly in recovery are common hires. For the professionals, hiring therapists new to the field and physicians with disreputable backgrounds or little experience treating addiction cases saves a lot of money. So does using unpaid Marriage and Family Therapist interns who facilitate both individual and group therapy, as well as utilizing the support staff to document clinical hours. As mentioned above, serving low-quality cafeteria style food is another common cost-cutting strategy.

In California, the RADT 1 certification is the lowest, most entry-level certification a treatment employee can get and be eligible to document billable clinical hours spent with a patient. This is an important point to consider for a few reasons. First, the RADT 1 certification is trivial; it is a simple 9-hour course administered either in person or online, consisting of three hours each of ethics, professional boundaries, and confidentiality. There is no way a person with just this certification should be allowed to bill for "clinical" time spent with individuals.

During my stint as an operations director, the

owners I worked for wanted me and my entire support staff to become RADT 1 certified so we could all start documenting billable clinical hours. I signed up for what I anticipated would be this 9-hour course, only to complete and pass the certification test in 45 minutes. With my new certification, I was now qualified, according to the State of California, to run and document group therapy sessions eligible for insurance reimbursement. Within a couple of weeks of my completion of the RADT 1, most of my staff had completed theirs as well, and the owners had them running groups like "Mindful Walks" (taking walks through the neighborhood), and "Movie Therapy" (watching dvd's), and then submitting the documented hours for reimbursement. The owners were capturing thousands of dollars billing for group therapy led by $12 per hour techs who did not have college degrees or any counseling experience. Needless to say, none of these groups provided any therapeutic benefit to the patients, but it didn't matter, as the owners were getting paid.

Owners will gladly pay for their support staff to get the RADT 1 because it's a very cheap way to document billable clinical hours. Tech's make $10-$15 an hour versus a therapist who can command as much as ten times that amount. Remember, the name of the game from the owner's perspective is to document the *minimum* number of clinical hours each day (per patient) required to capture insurance reimbursement as cheaply as possible. In California, this ruse has become common practice, especially amongst rehabs in the Orange County area.

Please be mindful of this if you are researching rehab facilities in California. Ask if they use RADT 1 certified staff to run therapeutic groups. If they say yes, ask if those staff members are also licensed therapists, or at the very least if they possess additional certifications like a CADC or a CATC. If they do not, find another facility. Remember, make sure to get your answers in writing. Owners and intake salesmen are notorious for lying and misrepresenting their services and clinical programming.

Many individuals who work in the treatment field are in recovery themselves, in particular support staff employees who, in my opinion, are too unqualified to be working in treatment unless they have, at a minimum, one to two years of continual abstinence. The traditional rule of thumb is that a person must have at least one year of continual abstinence before they can be hired to work in a treatment setting. This is by no means a law; it is just a general guideline that many treatment centers abide by, but it's not always the case. In fact, there seems to be a trend to hire support staff who have substantially less sober time than a year, with many of these hires being former opioid addicts (the group with the highest probability to relapse).

People newly in recovery tend to gravitate towards

the treatment field because they want to give something back, which is commendable. But they also often desire to be in an environment supportive of their own fledgling recovery, which may not be the best for you or your loved one to be around recent addicts. Owners like hiring these individuals because they usually do not need to pay them much, and among the newly abstinent, many are grateful just to have a job. In certain cases, owners will also barter with the person, offering free room and board, and a few bucks a week in exchange for their labor. The owners get to reduce their costs by not having to pay much for labor, and the former-addict tech gets a free place to live.

There are many good reasons why hiring qualified support staff is critical to a patient's success, but the most important is patients spend most of their time interacting with the support staff, compared to time with professional clinicians and therapists. Addicts going through treatment are very susceptible to programming, so it is vital that they are surrounded by individuals who are healthy and of the highest integrity. There was a recent incident in Pennsylvania where two rehab employees overdosed on heroin and fentanyl while at work, only to be discovered dead by the very patients whom they were employed to be supervising. A similar incident occurred only a few weeks later at a sober-living facility in Malibu. One of the employees, an individual newly in recovery but who had a long history of chronic relapse, overdosed on heroin. With only a few month's clean time, he had been offered free room and board in exchange for supervising clients up to 40 hours a week. On the day of the overdose, he disappeared into his bedroom mid-shift, shot up, died, and was later found by one of the clients staying in the house. I can only imagine how upsetting and triggering such instances as these are for the clients who found these staff members deceased due to a drug overdose. The story gets worse, though. His replacement was another individual new to recovery who was offered free room and board in exchange for labor. That person was fired on his second week for sleeping with not one, but two female clients while he was at work.

Examples like these are just a few of the reasons why it is important to do some due diligence into any facility you are considering. Ask the intake person you speak to questions like: who is on the support staff, are they in recovery themselves, how much clean time do they have, how long have they worked there, and what their drugs of choice were (they probably won't be able to answer this question but it doesn't hurt to ask).

In many treatment settings, it is also the techs who are responsible to oversee medication dispensing. I cannot stress how crucial this is. Make sure that whichever treatment center you or your loved one goes to, they have at least one qualified nurse on each shift (typically 3 shifts per 24 hour period, morning, mid-day, overnight) who is in charge of observing the medications being dispensed. Medication errors occur frequently (even by nurses), and because there is a propensity by treatment centers to hire unqualified, low wage, poorly-trained staff who have a hard time discerning medication orders, patient fatalities can and do occur.[10]

There are far more smaller facilities than larger institutions. Because of this reality, the smaller facilities tend to fly under the radar a little easier than their larger counterparts with regards to fraudulent urine, DNA and allergy testing scams, body brokering, and self-referrals that are all common insurance fraud practices within the industry. The detox facility I ran was a small 6-bed facility, and the owners I worked for routinely engaged in all of these practices. The clinical director was forced to falsely document therapy sessions with patients that were never provided, simply because the owners refused to hire enough clinical staff necessary to provide the insurance mandated clinical hours. In fact, after I left, the individual who replaced me told me the owners had him go back into the electronic medical record system to document over 40 hours of clinical programming that had never been

---

[10] "American Addiction Centers: Even More Undisclosed Deaths, Jerrod Menz Indicted for Murder, and the Start of Real Problems," *Bleeker Street* Research, August 4, 2015, http://bleeckerstreetresearch.com/2015/08/american-addiction-centers-even-more-undisclosed-deaths-jerrod-menz-indicted-for-murder-and-the-start-of-real-problems/

provided to certain patients just so the owners could show the necessary clinical hours to capture reimbursement for those patients. This was a facility that advertised art and music therapy on their website, when the truth was they didn't even offer basic services like chemical dependency counseling (mandatory in residential treatment).

Another form of insurance fraud common within the industry is for rehab centers to bill for treatment benefits they are not entitled to. For example, one facility I worked at started out as a detox-only facility, but then transitioned to a residential treatment facility after the owners realized they weren't making enough money by offering just detox services. When a patient's detox benefits were either denied or cut off, the owners would start billing for their residential treatment center (RTC) benefits without providing the patients with the therapeutic hours required to capture RTC reimbursement. This practice continued even when the RTC benefits were denied, as they would start billing for partial hospitalization treatment programs (PHP) or intensive outpatient (IOP) treatment when they legally not allowed to bill for either. By doing this, the owners were eating away at all the possible insurance benefits a patient could get, yet not providing a single bit of the therapy the patient desperately needed.

Larger facilities or facilities that are in the "business of treatment" tend to offer the whole chain of services—detox, RTC, PHP or IOP, and sober living—so be aware of this while you are doing your research, as they typically are profit motivated and may be tempted to play the billing game I've just described. Both large and small treatment facilities are equally capable at cheating insurers out of benefits you are entitled to if they so choose, so it is imperative to keep track of all the therapeutic programming you receive while in treatment.

Anytime an individual or institution seeks reimbursement from your health insurance, your health insurance company will send you an EOB (explanation of benefits), which outlines what the service or treatment was, how much the medical provider was seeking in compensation, what your insurance company agreed to pay them, and what portion the patient is responsible for. Make sure you match up the therapeutic programming you receive in treatment to the EOB your insurance company sends you for all the therapy and medical services the facility is seeking reimbursement for while you were in their care. There should absolutely be no discrepancies between the two, and if there is you should contact your insurance carrier to dispute it if you find that the treatment center was trying to bill for therapy you never received. Unfortunately, it has become an all too common occurrence for treatment centers to seek reimbursement for services never rendered.

Let me add that there is something to be said about having solid documentation and professional billing experience when it comes to getting benefits approved for insurance payments. If your insurance covers detox and rehab, you need to be sure the facility knows how to do the proper billing for the services provided. It is supposed to be a collaboration between the therapists and clinicians at the treatment facility, and the billers who work for the billing company. In this regard, it is good to find out how long any treatment center you are considering has been in business. This will give you an idea as to how many patients they have seen through the years, and what their level of expertise is with getting treatment benefits approved. Make sure you ask what steps the facility will take if your health insurance company denies your benefits or drops you to a lower level of care the facility is unable to provide. Will they bill for residential treatment (RTC) if you are still detoxing and your insurance company denies detox benefits? Find out how many residential treatment days they typically get approved for their patients before they are stepped down to lower levels of care (it varies but the answer will give you an idea of what to expect).

It is not uncommon for a patient's benefits to run out before their program is completed. If your benefits run out while you are in treatment, find out what steps the facility will take on your behalf. Will they kick you out, will they cover the cost of the remaining treatment, will they refer you to a sober living or an IOP program? Unfortunately, it is not an uncommon practice for a treatment center to give a patient just 24 hours' notice to either come up with the money to pay for their remaining treatment or be asked to leave. Please be sure to have a contingency plan in place in case this happens to you, and make sure you get your preadmission answers in writing, especially if they tell you they will cover the remaining cost of your treatment if your benefits get cut off before the end of your treatment stay.

One additional point to make here is that it is not uncommon for a patient to go out and relapse if they know their benefits are running out and they do not have a place to go. If they can produce a dirty urine test, either with their own urine or using someone else's, the treatment facility, IOP or PHP program can submit the test to the insurance company as proof of relapse, and the insurance company will then be forced to reset the patients benefits, starting the treatment process all over again at square one. It is not the most honorable thing to do but if the patient's only other option is getting kicked out on the street, staying in treatment is clearly a more desirable alternative.

The Business of treatment with ancillary services

The introduction of insurance benefits into the treatment world spurned the development of three highly lucrative sub-industries: body brokering, the billing of Medical Lab Services, and for JCAHO and CARF, the business of accreditation.

Body brokering is a term associated with "selling" addicts to treatment centers in return for a placement fee. Obviously, this isn't a form of slavery, as no one is actually "sold" to a treatment center, but a patient's insurance benefits are.

How this typically works is like this. Let's say I have a relationship with a treatment center that will pay me $5000 for every client I send them who stays for at least two weeks. Two weeks is a benchmark because the facility needs to bill 14 overnight stays to justify cutting the body broker a $5000 referral check, yet still make a huge amount of money. Treatment centers bill for each night stayed; days in treatment do not count for residential treatment reimbursement. Since I know the facility will pay me for each client I send them who stays for at least the minimum time, I'm going to do whatever I can to recruit addicts. I'll go to local 12-step meetings, drive into drug infested areas, network with therapists and doctors, advertise free treatment on Craigslist....you name it and I'm doing it. I don't even care if the person wants to get sober or if they have insurance, I will buy it for them if they do not have it. I will gladly spend the $500, $600 or $700 premium to buy them a month's worth of health insurance just to get them into treatment. It's a small cost of doing business. I will give them $500 to $1000 if they stay at least two weeks, and I will even pay for their plane ticket to get to treatment (if it's out of state). Even better, I will give them another $500 if, while they are in treatment, they recruit other patients by getting them to agree to leave treatment, relapse, and then enter another facility I also have a relationship with. I will then pay that second client $500 to $1000 to do exactly what the first client did. You might be asking: "Does this really happen?" Yes, it does! I have witnessed it first-hand.

I have worked at facilities where body brokers were employed to steer clients into detox and treatment. In one instance, the broker, who was located in the Midwest, would advertise free treatment on Craigslist. The areas he sourced patients from were severely impoverished, and most of the individuals could not afford health insurance. This body broker would offer to pay for their health insurance and their plane ticket to California in exchange for their commitment to stay at least two weeks. Why would someone agree to go into treatment if they did not want to get sober? The answer is, so many hard-core drug addicts today do not have a place to live, their own bed or food to eat. They are constantly having to come up with ways to score drugs (stealing, panhandling, prostitution, etc.). By offering an addict a free place to stay, free food, free pharmaceutical drugs, and money, why would they say no?

The most common way for body brokers to circumvent the open enrollment period is through a "qualifying life event." Qualifying life events include: loss of health insurance (excluding defaulting on your premiums), changes in household, changes in residence, becoming eligible for Medicaid, and for a few other noteworthy reasons. Changes in residence is the most prevalent way for body brokers to skirt open enrollment. Typically, they will enroll the patient in a health insurance policy using a fake address in the state or nearby city where they will be seeking treatment.

My advice to you is to be wary of anyone who claims to do "treatment placement." You really do not know what their motivations are. It is likely they are referring you to a facility with which they have a referral relationship, and not to a facility best suited for your needs. Personally, I have been approached by treatment center owners dozens of times with offers of $5,000 as client referral fees. I have never accepted a referral fee for treatment placement and I never will. It is a highly unethical and illegal practice that unfortunately is all too common in an industry filled with greedy and desperate treatment center owners. I even know of treatment centers owners who will pay for a patient's health insurance just to get them in, because once they're in, that's where real money can be made, as the subject coming up next will explain.

Liquid gold for treatment centers

Urine testing (commonly referred to as Liquid Gold), DNA testing, and allergy testing are by far some of the biggest scams in the rehab world. Rehab owners mandate that patients perform these tests for one reason only—they are a highly lucrative ancillary source of revenue. In fact, many treatment centers are only profitable because of their urine testing program. DNA testing has the potential to provide a benefit if the doctors actually review the results and adjust a patient's medications according to how they metabolize them. As for allergy testing, there is absolutely no place for it in rehab. Rehab doctors and owners only administer this test for the financial compensation they receive.

At the detox facility where I worked, the owners implemented DNA testing only because of the financial benefits they would receive. By the time the test results would come back, our patients were already 75% of the way through their detox and almost off of most of their medications, rendering these expensive tests almost useless. In longer term treatment settings, doctors and psychiatrists may have more time to alter their patients' medications based on the DNA test results, but only if they actually review them and understand how to interpret them.

In most treatment settings, patients will typically be urine tested anywhere from 3 to 7 times per week, using a 12-panel POC (point of care) test. The patient urinates into a cup and depending upon the substances they have in their system, the test will register as either positive or negative for the presence of a drug or narcotic associated with each panel (qualitative test). The drug panels on the most commonly used 12-panel urine drug tests measure for the presence of amphetamines, methamphetamines, barbiturates, benzodiazepines, marijuana, opiates, cocaine, phencyclidine (PCP), methadone, propoxyphene (opioid), MDMA (ecstasy), and extended opiates. Regardless of whether the POC test comes up positive or not, many rehabs will still send the samples to a lab for a confirmation test (quantitative test), which measures for specific substances and their amount.

When the lab runs the confirmation test, they will bill the patient's insurance for that test, but the patient (or their family depending on whose policy it is) can often receive huge bills from the lab for the fees the health insurance doesn't cover. Sometimes the fees for urine testing, depending on how long a person is in treatment for (detox, residential, PHP, IOP, sober living) and how frequently they are tested, are greater than the cost of treatment itself. It is not uncommon for a person to receive a bill in the hundreds of thousands of dollars for these unnecessary tests.[11] Can

---

[11] Pat Beall, "Addiction treatment bonanza: How urine tests rake in millions," *My Palm Beach Post*, August 1, 2015,

you imagine how shocking it would be to leave treatment only to come home to a lab bill requiring you to pay tens of thousands or even a hundred thousand dollars in fees for a medical service that in no way added to the efficacy of your treatment or supported your ability to create a sober life for yourself?

You may be wondering how someone could get stuck with such a huge lab bill. Here's a scenario to show how easily it happens. Say an individual starts out in detox for a week, steps down to residential treatment for 30 to 90 days, and then transitions into a sober living house while attending an IOP program for six months. They are tested three to seven times per week, every week, and each one of those tests is sent to a lab for confirmation. Over the course of that 9-month period, you are looking at anywhere from 108 to 252 drug tests. Each confirmation test can be billed out for thousands of dollars, as it all depends on how much the lab decides to bill the insurance company. In our example, let's assume the lab bills the health insurance company $5,000 per test. Let's assume your health insurance policy allows only 50% of the fee, $2500, so your liability for the uncollected billing portion could be as much as $270,000 to $630,000. As insane as this sounds, it happens! These medical tests are just one of

---

http://www.mypalmbeachpost.com/news/addiction-treatment-bonanza-how-urine-tests-rake-millions/rvmrD8VMBwykDtd6TCSALJ/

the many reasons why everyone's health insurance premiums are skyrocketing, and yet these tests in no way whatsoever do anything to benefit the health of the patient.

You may be wondering how treatment centers themselves make money off of lab services. After all, it appears that the labs are the ones profiting from the system. This is a legal grey area that falls under the federal Stark Laws, which were designed to protect patients against the practice of self-referral, but which seem to carry different interpretations depending on the state the lab resides in. Some rehabs will bill and collect on the point of care test (the initial urine screening) as a way to recoup their out-of-pocket costs for the test cups. Typically, a health insurance company is billed only about $10 per panel for the initial POC test, thus $120 total for a 12-panel test (front-end billing).

But the lucrative portion of the urine testing games lies in the confirmation or quantitative test performed at the lab (back-end billing). So how does a detox facility, rehab facility, a PHP, IOP or a sober living benefit from the fees charged for the confirmation testing? Follow the money game, of course. Since the passing of the Affordable Care Act, the lab business has exploded, and many lab owners have hired salesmen to find referrals to push their services. Also, seeing the potential to tap into the rehab industry to take advantage of the exploding opioid epidemic and the endless stream of insurance dollars, labs began selling equity interests in their businesses to owners of treatment centers, IOP's, PHP's and sober living facilities so the owners could collect on a portion of the highly lucrative quantitative test, while the lab gets a steady stream of testing to perform! It's a win-win situation for both the rehab facility owners and the labs.

When I owned a sober living facility in Malibu, I was approached by a lab owner who offered to have me buy into his lab. For my $10,000 investment, I would own a piece of the lab and would be able to receive money on both the front-end and back-end collections of every sample I sent for confirmation testing. The more samples I sent, the more money I would make; pretty simple. Seeing the moral (and potentially) legal dilemma of his proposition, I rejected his offer. For many other owners, however, the temptation to take advantage of this potentially lucrative revenue stream is too hard to resist. The first time I met the owner and CEO of the detox facility I ran, he bragged to me how he had made over $300,000 the year before in just urine testing alone. But not a single one of those tests did anything to improve the health and wellness of the patient who had to pay for it.

It is preposterous to be urine testing anyone more than twice while they are in treatment, unless they are suspected of using or if at some point during their stay they left the property unsupervised and later returned.

It is understandable to be tested upon admission to show the presence of drugs in a person's system. A dirty drug test is one of the prerequisites insurance companies will require before they release treatment benefits. It is also understandable, but by no means required, to test a person again before they leave to show there are no drugs present in the body.

All patients are searched upon admission, both their person as well as their luggage. If patients are getting high while in treatment it is up to the facility to do a better job of controlling and monitoring their environment, and the cost of which should not be passed onto the patient in the form expensive urine tests.

Drugs such as marijuana can trigger a positive drug test for up to a month after a person uses, so it is silly to test a person multiple times a week when it's a given that drugs are still in their system. It is even more ridiculous to repeatedly test a person and send each and every sample for confirmation. Can you imagine a person entering treatment for alcohol being tested 3-7 times a week for drugs they have never taken, and then having to pay for those unnecessary tests? It happens every day in rehabs across the country!

Lab tests are medical tests. A doctor's signature is required on the lab requisition form and a doctor has to be able to justify that the test is medically necessary. But there is absolutely no justifiable medical necessity to drug test a person in treatment multiple times a week. Doctors do not adjust a patient's detox or medication schedule based on existing levels of a substance in their patients' urine. Treatment centers, IOP's, PHP's and sober livings engage in this practice solely for the obscene amounts of money they earn from over-testing. Grant it IOP's and PHP's are off-site forms of treatment so it makes sense to randomly urine test patients. But what does not make sense is to make it a practice to send negative POC tests to a lab for confirmation.

For any facility you consider, make sure to ask how often you will be urine tested, what other tests they will run and submit to your insurance company, do they submit negative POC tests for confirmation, and ask if you can opt out. If they tell you multiple weekly urine tests are part of their program, find another place to go.

As for labs, if you happen to go to a facility that engages in these practices and you get stuck with a large bill for unnecessary testing services, dispute the charges with the lab and refuse to pay them. The insurance company has reimbursed for a portion of the test, but the lab may try to pass along the remaining portion to the policy holder. If you get a bill, tell the lab you are not going to pay. The lab may threaten to send you to collections or to sue, but it's an empty threat. The lab will have to disclose their billing practices, which typically are not in line with the insurance company fee schedule and probably border on the illegal.

An important fact to be aware of with regards to sober living facilities is that it is illegal for them to engage in urine testing for profit, as well as to receive cash kickbacks from treatment centers, IOP's and PHP's for housing patients. Sober livings are, by definition, unlicensed facilities, and they cannot provide or engage in any sort of medical service. However, beware: it is common in California and Florida for sober living owners to establish quid pro quo financial relationships with rehabs, IOP and PHP programs. The way it works is as follows.

First, IOP and PHP programs are outpatient therapeutic programs commonly located in a commercial office building, separate from residential treatment. Because California and Florida receive so many out of state patients, there is a demand for residential housing where patients can stay when their residential treatment benefits run out. In order to capture the IOP or PHP benefits, treatment centers, IOP's and PHP's refer patients to sober living facilities where they can live while the patient continues on with their therapeutic program. Because insurance does not pay for sober living, the IOP, PHP or treatment center will pay for sober living out of the collections they receive from the patients' health insurance policy for the IOP or PHP treatment. The treatment center, IOP or PHP will bill the patient's insurance for treatment and urine testing, and pay a fee back to the sober living owner for housing the patient.

Technically speaking, this is not a bad thing for the patient if both the sober living and the IOP or PHP program are reputable. But again, please do your due diligence on both environments before committing. Many sober living homes are over-crowded with three to four beds to a room, and drug use is a common occurrence within these unregulated environments. And their arrangement with the treatment center or IOP/PHP may encourage excessive urine testing to generate revenues.

If you are thinking about going to a sober living after treatment, make sure you find out if they implement a urine testing program that sends the tests to a lab for confirmation. Sober livings can and do mandate point of care urine tests to make sure their clients are not using, which is perfectly normal and recommended. However, they absolutely are not allowed to send the samples to a lab for confirmation or receive money for doing so.

As mentioned, keep in mind also some of the larger facilities own their own labs. If a treatment center owns their own lab, find somewhere else to seek treatment because this means they are likely in the treatment business just for the money. A common scam that treatment centers employ is to offer free follow-up treatment if you stay for 90-days but relapse within a year. As a rule, these facilities can do this because they employ aggressive urine testing practices and make enough money off their lab testing to offer the free relapse treatment. If you decide to admit into a facility that offers such free relapse care, make sure you find out if the offer includes free urine testing as well. I doubt it, but if by chance they say it does, get it in writing so you can hold them accountable.

A Facility's Accreditations Don't Mean Squat

You may be asking what are accreditations and what do they have to do with treatment? The answer is actually "very little." But that doesn't stop treatment centers from flaunting accreditations and "seals of approval" on their websites to give the appearance that the facility is somehow superior to others that do not possess the same.

First of all, know that some accreditations are, in fact, simply purchased. For example, the National Association of Addiction Treatment Providers (NAATP), while noble in its mission, sells a membership that treatment centers, for a fee, can become affiliated with. Once they pay, they can use NAATP's "seal of approval" on their website to give the appearance of credibility and professionalism when in fact the endorsement was purchased.

In the U.S., the two accreditations that treatment centers most commonly seek are The Joint Commission on Accreditation of Healthcare Organizations (JCAHO) and the Commission on Accreditation of Rehabilitation Facilities (CARF), both of which primarily accredit hospitals and organizations working in the human services field. Many treatment centers will get either one or the other, and some will get both. JCAHO accreditation is recognized as "the gold standard" of accreditation, and the process of attaining it is arduous, time consuming, and expensive. Less so for a CARF accreditation. (A paradox that I expose in my upcoming book is that JCAHO played a direct role in furthering America's opioid crisis, yet they are the "gold standard" of accreditations.)

Treatment centers that go through the accreditation process do so for one reason only—to capture insurance reimbursement from as many insurance companies as possible. But there is absolutely no provable correlation between accreditation and the efficacy of treatment, none! Treatment centers misleadingly advertise their accreditations in ways that give the appearance they are somehow superior to those that have not undergone the process. In fact, one of the most expensive residential treatment centers in the country uses their JCAHO accreditation to falsely advertise they are among a selective 6% of treatment centers "to earn this honor," when in fact the percentage of JCAHO accredited treatment centers is considerably higher.[12]

---

[12] "Facts about Behavioral Health Care Accreditation," *The Joint Commission,* November 18, 2016, http://www.jointcommission.org/facts_about_behavioral_health_care_accreditation/

The only honor in attaining an accreditation is making it through the accreditation process, which is a painstakingly time-consuming bureaucratic ordeal during which the center's physical plant, professional staff, and methodologies are assessed according to certain standards. The problem is, there is no standard for the success rate itself in any of these accreditations. Moreover, the accreditation processes itself causes treatment center employees nothing but stress. They create mountains of tedious and mundane layers of paperwork, which pull staff attention away from where it matters most—on client care.

Even after the facility receives an accreditation, they are burdened by ongoing processes the accrediting body requires to maintain a "seal of approval." The only thing these added processes do is take time and attention away from client care. Neither JCAHO nor CARF can provide a single shred of evidence that their accreditations improve the efficacy or effectiveness of treatment or the environment in which it is facilitated. They cannot demonstrate that their processes improve the safety of the clients who the facilities are mandated to serve. Finally, these accreditations in no way ensure successful or improved treatment outcomes.

The push for accreditation occurred when the insurance industry entered the treatment world. A common phenomenon in the medical business is that as soon as health insurance companies are mandated to cover an illness, they will do whatever possible to find ways to deny coverage. The motive behind this is obvious. Insurance companies want to hold onto as much of your premium dollars as possible, without having to pay out for medical treatments and services you may need or are entitled to.

One way health insurance companies are able to deny treatment benefits for substance abuse and mental health services is to limit the number of providers eligible to receive reimbursement. In the case of substance abuse treatment, the easiest method to deny benefits is to limit payments only to those treatment centers that are JCAHO or CARF accredited. When health insurance providers were first mandated to cover substance abuse treatment benefits, only a relatively small number of treatment centers were accredited, so denying coverage was common. This meant that the health insurance companies were able to keep most of your premium. Over time, as treatment centers became wise to the scheme, they jumped on the accreditation bandwagon just so they would become eligible to receive reimbursement from a greater number of health insurance companies. While this makes profit sense, it still does not signify that accredited facilities are better than non-accredited ones.

What we are witnessing now as more and more facilities become accredited is a dilution of the value of having a seal of approval. Nevertheless, once treatment centers receive their accreditations, they proudly and prominently display the symbolic seal on the homepage of their website, suggesting reputability and superiority.

Keep in mind that the process of attaining and maintaining both JCAHO and CARF accreditations are expensive and laborious. This creates a barrier for the smaller facilities to become accredited because they simply do not have the same financial resources that larger, more expensive treatment conglomerates possess.

As an example of how accreditations do not ensure patient safety or higher quality outcomes, while working at the detox facility, to put it mildly, the owners I worked for had a rather "flexible" moral compass that ranged from slightly unethical to outright criminal. Right before I left the company, they decided to get JCAHO accreditation for the detox facility, as well as for their treatment center which is in a different part of the state some 200 miles away. The only reason for the accreditation was so they could capture higher rates of reimbursement, and to open themselves up to receiving reimbursement from additional health insurers.

During my time there, as well as after I had left, the company routinely engaged in various forms of insurance fraud, including documenting and billing for clinical hours never provided to clients, billing for medical services never rendered, and paying referral fees to "body brokers" for sending them clients. During the accreditation process, which occurred after I had left, I caught wind from the individual who took over my position that the company was still engaging in these very same activities. At no point during JCAHO's audit did they catch any of these criminal transgressions. In fact, when it came down to the final walk-through of the detox facility, JCAHO never even showed up. Instead, they visited the treatment center, and signed off on the detox facility's accreditation without completing its final walk-through.

Accreditations are nothing more than hollow stamps on a website. Their processes are supposed to be designed to ensure that the internal mechanisms of running a business in the health services field occur in a very particular way, and they typically involve many additional layers of paperwork resulting in compliance oversight. Treatment centers advertise their accreditations in illusory ways to influence potential patients into thinking their programs are superior to non-accredited ones when in fact they do nothing to ensure that clients remain properly cared for, or that insurance fraud and other nefarious criminal activities do not occur. The agencies backing these accreditations are a business, albeit nonprofit, whose interests lie in approving whichever facility chooses to undergo the process because there are substantial fees involved.13 This system is no different than what occurred during the subprime crisis when the bond rating agencies were selling AAA ratings to subprime mortgage debt issuers without even bothering to check on the quality of the bond offerings.

The takeaway here: Accreditations Don't Mean Squat! Do not be fooled by the seals of approval that many treatment centers promote in their marketing materials and on their websites. In no way does accreditation or membership in any of these associations guarantee that you will receive effective treatment. Nor does it guarantee against insurance fraud, patient neglect, the excessive use of unnecessary billable medical tests and services, and the worst case of all, patient fatality. Please refer back to the questions that you should ask that I outlined in the previous chapter, and if you can, always tour the facility first to see for yourself where either you or your loved one will be going.

Conflict of Interest

One last point I would like to make with regards to the industry as a whole. There is an embedded conflict of interest in residential treatment centers that pits

---

13 "The Skinny on TJC Accreditation," *BHM Healthcare Solutions, http://bhmpc.com/2014/09/the-skinny-on-tjc-accreditation*

successful treatment against profit. A facility may say they want to see you healed and free of addiction, but, on the other hand, it's a given that they would love you to come back as a "repeat customer." This is even more true today with health insurance regulations barring denial of benefits due to a pre-existing condition. The majority of individuals who seek treatment (especially for opioids) will relapse. Professionals in the industry commonly cite a 90% relapse rate among individuals who seek help for their addiction at a residential treatment facility.

Treatment center owners know this, and why wouldn't they love it? If you knew that you could make far more money by offering ineffective treatment than you could by offering treatment that worked, what would you do? Given the general lack of integrity that exists among rehab center owners within this industry, the answer is pretty clear. Maybe this is why the relapse rate is so high? Think about it.

The fact is, many relapsing clients will return back to the most recent treatment center they came from if they had a pleasant experience. They already know the routines and what to expect (staff, schedule, etc.), which is an added comfort level for them. And when they go back, how often do you think the facility holds itself responsible for failing their patient by offering ineffective treatment? Never. When patients return to treatment after a relapse, they will usually hear statements like: "You must not have worked your

Drug Rehab

program hard enough," "You didn't go to enough meetings," and "You didn't want it badly enough." It's never, "We didn't give you the tools necessary for you to create a sober life upon discharge," "We didn't heal your underlying physiological and psychological drivers of addiction," "Our clinical programming fell short," "The medications we discharged you on triggered your relapse," or "We didn't provide you with the understanding of what addiction is, and how the society in which we live promotes an addicted state of consciousness."

Ultimately, the decision to relapse or to stay sober comes down to how each person chooses to exercise his or her divine right of free will. But if you are set free with an anchor tethered to your leg, chances are you're going to drown.

The hidden gems of treatment

As compared to larger institutional facilities, smaller facilities within the treatment world are, in my view, the "hidden gems" of treatment. Often more expensive than their larger counterparts, these types of facilities have a propensity to display a genuine care for their patients, placing treatment outcomes ahead of profits. They offer more personalized levels of care and therapeutic programming because the staff-to-client ratios are higher. This reduces the chances of a client slipping through the cracks. (Note by the way that

75

many facilities advertise high staff-to-client ratios, but they fail to disclose what types of staff members they include in those numbers. Are they counting the drivers, housekeepers, kitchen help, administrative staff and support staff members, because while these roles are important, these individuals typically do not add a whole lot of therapeutic value to the clinical program. So be sure you understand who is included when comparing staff-to-client ratios.)

Smaller rehabs tend to have more of a family feel to them, though not always. I cannot stress enough how important it is to visit the facility for yourself prior to admitting. On a visit, you will be able to see firsthand how well the facility is maintained, how the staff interacts with the patients, and how the patients present themselves (look for signs to see if they're overmedicated). You can speak with the clinical and support staff, check out the clinical schedule, the activity schedule, the menus, and hopefully meet with the owner(s).

High-quality facilities do exist, but the industry unfortunately lacks any sort of performance ranking system. It is cloaked in fraudulent advertising and misinformation that is very difficult to weed out. That is why it is vitally important to do the due diligence for yourself before you commit to any facility. Ask the questions I have suggested in these chapters. Do a Google search on the facility, the owners, the clinical staff, and the doctors affiliated with the program to make sure they have not been put on probation by their medical board or had their license suspended or revoked. Also, search to see if any patient fatalities have occurred at the facility. Treatment centers have a tendency to not report patient fatalities, but disgruntled clients and staff sometimes post this information on the Internet.

People researching treatment centers often spend more time researching their next car versus which treatment center either they or their loved one will go to. Don't be one of those people! All rehabs are not the same, so make sure you do your homework!

A final point that I feel is important to make here is there is nothing wrong with a facility earning a profit. The operational costs of running a high-quality treatment program are high, and certainly employees and owners have the right to earn a living. What is inherently wrong with the industry as a whole is that it has become motivated to profit off of human suffering that in large part has been created by the pharmaceutical industry. And the desire to capture those profits is exponentially greater than the desire to achieve positive treatment outcomes, which I might add, have not substantially improved since the first treatment center opened its doors some 60 years ago.

#3 – Medications Are Not the Complete Answer

I am not a doctor, nor will I be dispensing any medical advice regarding specific medications. The goal of this chapter is simply to convey general information on how medications are utilized in addiction treatment today, the types of medications most commonly prescribed (excluding antidepressants), what to be aware of and watch out for, and some questions you might want to ask in advance of admitting. I will also include an example of medication orders and a taper schedule for an opioid detox used by a physician I have worked with extensively. She has successfully detoxed thousands of patients during her career as the medical director of several rehab and detox facilities in Malibu, California, and the medication orders and taper schedule are her standard opioid detox protocol. These are examples only; adjustments to a patient's medication(s) and taper schedule must be made according to each individual patient assessment and corresponding lab results.

The medications I discuss are some of the more common medications used in residential detox and treatment settings, but this is by no means an exhaustive list. I would like to convey that many treatment doctors and psychiatrists have a propensity to start patients out immediately on antidepressants when they first enter treatment if they hear patients say they are depressed. My answer to that is "of course they are." People don't become addicted to drugs and alcohol because they are happy. Many of the symptoms antidepressants are designed to manage can be corrected through simple dietary and lifestyle changes. In my experience working in the field with thought leaders who specialize in functional medicine and holistic psychiatry, these symptoms oftentimes do not warrant the use of pharmaceutical medications.

Western medication has become the "go to" tool used in most treatment centers today. This makes sense. Once health insurance started providing benefits to treat substance abuse and mental health disorders, it paved the way for a mountainous supply of pharmaceutical drugs to follow. In fact, insurance companies encourage treatment facilities to push medications, especially in the case of opioid addiction. It is far more profitable for an insurance carrier to have their policy holders physically addicted to pharmaceutical medications designed to block the physical cravings of opioids than it is to provide benefits for repeat treatment visits following a relapse.

Opioid abuse medications

The most common pharmaceutical drugs used to treat opioid addiction are methadone, buprenorphine (Subutex), buprenorphine and naloxone (Suboxone) and naltrexone (Vivitrol). These are usually used in combination with other drugs to manage the physical and psychological symptoms of opioid withdrawal.

Methadone, available as a liquid, pill, or sublingual tablet, is an opioid that blocks the "high" associated with using heroin or other prescription opioids. It works by binding itself to the same receptors on the brain that heroin and prescription opioids do, but without causing the euphoric effects associated with heroin or prescription opioids. It also reduces the cravings and withdrawal symptoms caused by opioid use. There are some significant shortcomings associated with methadone. One, it is physically addicting and it carries a high risk of abuse. Two, it typically is administered once a day at a clinic, which can be a huge inconvenience to anyone with a job, family, or a person who wants to travel. Three, like buprenorphine and naltrexone, methadone is only a drug substitute that does not heal the underlying drivers of addiction. Four, detoxing off of methadone is a painfully brutal experience. The drug is designed to merely manage the physical cravings and withdrawal symptoms of opioid addiction, nothing more.

Buprenorphine is a "sticky," partial opioid

antagonist most commonly administered sublingually either through a film, tablet or a patch. What this means is that it sticks to the opioid receptors in the brain very well, bumping other opioid drugs out of the same receptors and eliminating their euphoric effects while simultaneously satisfying the physical cravings of opioid addiction. Naloxone is an opiate antagonist that acts as an abuse deterrent to prevent patients from injecting the drug by sending them into a state of precipitated withdrawal if injected or used in conjunction with other opioids.

Suboxone and Subutex differ in that Suboxone contains two active ingredients (buprenorphine and naloxone) while Subutex contains one (buprenorphine). Because of the abuse deterrent properties of naloxone, most detox and treatment facilities will use Suboxone instead of Subutex. Other types of buprenorphine and naloxone (BupNx) medications include Zubsolv (sublingual) and Bunavail (buccal). In 2016, a buprenorphine subdermal implant called Probuphine was approved by the FDA, which is designed to deliver a steady dose of buprenorphine over a six-month period.

Naltrexone, administered as either a pill or an injection, is an FDA approved medication used to treat both opioid and alcohol use disorders. The mechanism of naltrexone is different from buprenorphine and methadone in that it binds to and blocks opioid receptors versus activating them. As such, it carries no risk of abuse or diversion. As a pill, it is typically administered once a day, and as an injection it is administered by a doctor once a month. To reduce the risk of precipitated withdrawal, patients are instructed to abstain from using opioids for 7 to 10 days prior to starting naltrexone.

The pros and cons of pharmaceutical drugs

There are benefits to using pharmaceutical drugs in treatment settings. The potential for adverse drug reactions and/or abuse can be negated when administered under the supervision of a qualified addiction medical specialist. And when you do not have to deal with physical cravings or withdrawal symptoms of opioid addiction, a patient will, theoretically, have an easier time engaging in therapy at the start of treatment.

But there are downsides to these medications as well. One, drugs that contain buprenorphine, or buprenorphine and naloxone are extremely hard to get off of. I have friends who, unfortunately, have been on them for years, want to get off of them, and are unable to taper themselves off. Long-term Suboxone use has been associated with depression, suicide, muscle and joint pain, loss of libido, anxiety, fatigue, nausea, and even psychosis. Many Suboxone users have claimed it is harder to get off of Suboxone than it is for heroin or OxyContin because Suboxone stays in the body longer than those two substances.[14] Third, like methadone, buprenorphine, naloxone, and naltrexone are merely substitutes for opioids. With the exception of naltrexone, they are all highly addicting in their own right, and they do not heal the underlying drivers of addictive behavior.

With long-term buprenorphine use, the drug dealer gets replaced by a doctor who the patient will need to see every 4-6 weeks to get the prescription refilled. As a word of caution, note that the market for illegal buprenorphine prescriptions is growing as street demand increases. Many doctors have recognized the financial opportunity in prescribing buprenorphine, opening up buprenorphine clinics that operate in similar morally questionable ways as did the illegal pill mills responsible for feeding America's opioid epidemic.[15]

In response, Congress passed the Drug Addiction Treatment Act in 2000 (DATA-2000), limiting the number of opioid abuse patients a doctor could treat with buprenorphine in their practice to 30. After just a year, doctors could apply for a waiver to increase the

---

[14] "The Dangers of Long Term Suboxone Use," *Maryland Addiction Recovery Center*, April 1, 2014, http://www.marylandaddictionrecovery.com/the-dangers-of-long-term-suboxone-use

[15] Deborah Sontag, "Addiction Treatment With a Dark Side," *The New York Times*, November 16, 2013, http://www.nytimes.com/2013/11/17/health/in-demand-in-clinics-and-on-the-street-bupe-can-be-savior-or-menace.html

number of opioid abuse patients from 30 to 100. Today, eligible doctors are allowed to prescribe buprenorphine to as many as 275 patients at a time once they possess the right waivers. There are many unscrupulous doctors practicing addiction medicine who know that once they have a patient on buprenorphine maintenance, the chances of them getting off of it are slim, and they will have a customer for a very long time.

In my view, drugs are an ever-present conflict of interest with Western medicine. Utilizing pharmaceutical drugs to manage symptoms has taken the place of healing the underlying drivers of poor health because there is far more money to be made maintaining a state of functional illness or disease. A doctor without a moral compass might easily ask: "Why would I ever taper off one of my buprenorphine patients when I know that for as long as they are on the drug, they will be a consistent source of income for me because they will be physically dependent upon my prescription pad?" The only other alternatives are to go cold turkey and deal with horrible withdrawal symptoms, or start abusing heroin or prescription narcotics again.

Of course, there are doctors who prescribe these drugs because they genuinely believe that a patient is better off on buprenorphine versus heroin or prescription opioid narcotics. But even when doctors sincerely feel this is true, they have to take into account the physical and psychological damage inherent with long-term buprenorphine maintenance and believe the risks associated with illicit drug use outweigh those of pharmaceutical substitutes. On this, I would disagree, having seen the physical and psychological damage that long-term use of buprenorphine causes.

Alcohol abuse medications

Some of the common medications used to treat alcohol abuse disorder are naltrexone (Vivitrol, ReVia), disulfiram (Antabuse), acamprosate (Campral), topiramate (Topamax), and baclofen (multiple drugs). During alcohol detox, doctors will commonly prescribe benzodiazepine's and anti-seizure medications (e.g. Keppra or Topamax) to combat withdrawal symptoms such as delirium tremens (DTs) and seizures. Alcohol detox differs from opioid detox in that a patient can die if the withdrawal symptoms are not medically supervised correctly, leading to seizures or respiratory arrest.

Naltrexone for alcohol abuse disorder reacts differently in the brain than it does for opioid abuse disorder in that a person on naltrexone who consumes alcohol can still feel the physical effects of the alcohol (impaired judgment, loss of coordination), but they will not experience the rewards or pleasure associated with drinking, making the experience less enjoyable. Vivitrol, the extended release formulation of naltrexone, appears to be the most effective form of the drug, as a single injection can last for as long as 30 days.

Disulfiram (Antabuse) is a medication designed to interfere with the body's ability to metabolize alcohol. If a person consumes alcohol while they are on Antabuse, they will experience severe nausea, flushing, and possibly heart palpitations. Disulfiram is not generally regarded as an effective tool to combat problem drinking because it works only when the patient takes the medication. So someone can take the drug Monday through Friday, but if they want to drink and party on Saturday night, they can simply not take the medication Saturday morning. Disulfiram is most effective being administered in a clinical setting by a doctor or a nurse, or when a spouse or loved one monitors the patient self-administering the medication as a way to ensure medication compliance.

Acamprosate (Campral) is a medication designed to decrease positive reinforcement of alcohol consumption and to reduce the symptoms associated with withdrawal. Research has shown Acamprosate can be an effective medication for those who have achieved abstinence from alcohol and would like to maintain it.

Topiramate (Topamax) in conjunction with having an anti-seizure indication, reduces the cravings for alcohol by suppressing the release of the neurotransmitter dopamine. The drug is reported to also have mood stabilizing properties so it is not uncommon for doctors to prescribe it to patients who present co-morbid psychiatric conditions.

Baclofen is used to reduce the rewarding, stimulating, and motivational properties associated with alcohol consumption, and has been shown to be effective against reducing the risk of relapse among at-risk or high-risk drinkers. Similar to topiramate, baclofen acts on the GABA receptors by reducing the craving for alcohol, while simultaneously reducing the withdrawal symptoms some experience when they quit drinking.

Another common class of drugs used in detox and treatment settings are benzodiazepine's. While it is true that these are highly addicting and frequently abused to the point that people enter treatment just to get off of them, they can be used to combat some of the physical (seizures) and psychological symptoms (anxiety) associated with withdrawal. Some of the more common benzodiazepines prescribed in treatment are Ativan, Valium, Serax, Xanax, Librium, Restoril, Rivotril, and Klonopin.

Cyclobenzaprine's (Flexeril, Amrix, Fexmid) are muscle relaxants, and another common class of drugs used in treatment and detox centers to manage the unpleasant physical symptoms of opioid withdrawal. They are not considered to be highly addicting but they can be misused, resulting in psychological dependency.

Sample medication order

One of my primary reasons for discussing medications and providing an example of medication orders and a taper schedule is to raise your awareness about being overprescribed medications while in treatment. I am not saying this is the norm, but it is not uncommon for patients to be overprescribed medications either due to the doctor's lack of experience or competence in the field of addiction medicine, or because the owners want to keep their patients in treatment for as long as the patients' insurance benefits will allow. The more medication prescribed and the more comfortable a patient is, the greater the chance they will stay longer in treatment.

There is generally a correlation between a patient's length of time in treatment and their ability to abstain from their drug(s) of choice upon discharge. But when a person is overmedicated, the efficacy of treatment decreases. Similar to being high on drugs or alcohol, when patients are overmedicated, they are unable to authentically access their emotions, and the work being done in therapy is negated. Emotional dysregulation is one of the primary drivers of addiction, so it is imperative that patients are able to learn how to access and process their emotions in healthy ways while free from the effects of mind and mood-altering substances.

The medication orders/taper schedule I have included on the following page was for a young male, mid-20's, who was an IV heroin and methamphetamine drug user who also abused benzodiazepines. In the year leading up to his arrival at detox, he had been injecting 1 to 2 grams of heroin a day, plus .5 grams to 1 gram of meth, and ingesting two to four milligrams of Xanax daily. His drug use was not outside the norm of most of the patients we received, and the doctor was able to detox him off of all controlled medications in 12 days. The following medications were ordered for his detox:

- Suboxone, 2mg strips for opioid withdrawal
- Klonopin, 1mg for anxiety and benzodiazepine withdrawal
- Robaxin, 750mg for muscle cramps associated with opioid withdrawal
- Seroquel, 50mg for anxiety and insomnia
- Phenergan, 25mg for severe nausea and vomiting associated with opioid withdrawal
- Clonidine, .1mg for bone pain or blood pressure greater than 160/100
- Imodium for diarrhea
- Melatonin, 3 to 6mg for insomnia

John Doe 9/16/92

3/19/16	Admit to detox
	Standing orders
	VS q 4 hrs while awake with COWS
	Notify me for BP greater than 170/110 or less than 90/50, HR greater than 140, RR greater than 24 or less than 10.
	Suboxone 2 mg strips
	May self-administer first test dose of Suboxone 2 mg SL x 1 when COWS= 13 or higher.
	If withdrawal symptoms are not made worse by test dose, then start:
	Suboxone 2 to 4 mg SL q 12 h NTE 8 mg/24 hrs (including test dose) (2 mg strips #30)
	Klonopin 1 mg, 1 to 2 mg po q 4-6 h prn anxiety- NTE 8 mg/24 hrs (#50)
	Robaxin 750 mg po q 6 hrs prn muscle cramps (#30)

	Seroquel 50 mg po TID prn anxiety and may have additional 50-100 mg po qhs prn insomnia Seroquel NTE 250 mg/24 hrs (50 mg tabs # 60) Separate Suboxone, Seroquel and Klonopin by at least 1 hour Phenergan 25 mg po q 6 hrs prn severe nausea/vomiting (#30) Clonidine 0.1 mg po q 6-8 h prn BP greater than 160/100 or bone pain, NTE 0.6 mg/24 hours (#30) Imodium 4 mg po prn loose stool, the 2 mg po prn each loose stool NTE 16 mg/24 hrs (1 box OTC pick up) Melatonin 3 to 6 mg po qhs prn insomnia OTC pick up Hold Suboxone, Clonindine, Seroquel and Klonopin for BP less than 100/60
3/20-3/22	Suboxone 2 to 4 mg SL q 12 h prn NTE 8 mg/24 hrs (including test dose)

3/23-3/25	Suboxone 2-3 mg SL q AM and 4 mg SL q PM prn NTE 7 mg
3/26	Suboxone 3 mg SL BID prn NTE 6 mg
3/27	Suboxone 2 mg SL q AM and 3 mg SL q PM prn NTE 5 mg
3/28	Suboxone 4 mg SL q day prn NTE 4
3/29	Suboxone 3 mg SL q day prn NTE 3
3/30	Suboxone 2 mg SL q day prn NTE 2
3/31	Suboxone 1 mg SL q day prn NTE 1
4/1	DC Suboxone
3/20-3/25	Klonopin 1 mg, 1 to 2 mg po q 4-6 h prn anxiety- NTE 8 mg/24 hrs (#50)
3/26	Klonopin 2 mg PO q AM, 1 mg PO midday, 2 mg PO evening, 2 mg PO q HS all prn NTE 7 mg
3/27	Klonopin 2 mg PO TID prn NTE 6 mg

3/28	Klonopin 2 mg PO q AM, 1 mg PO midday, 2 mg PO q PM all prn NTE 5 mg
3/29	Klonopin 2 mg PO BID prn NTE 4 mg
3/30	Klonopin 1 mg PO q AM and 2 mg PO q PM all prn NTE 3 mg
3/31	Klonopin 1 mg PO BID prn NTE 2
4/1	Klonopin 1 mg PO q day NTE 1
4/2	DC Klonopin

* The Medication Orders and Taper Schedule are for example only and not intended as medical advice or a schedule you should follow. Always consult with a qualified addiction specialist prior to beginning any drug or alcohol detoxification protocol.

While these orders may look complicated to the layperson, it is actually quite straightforward for a trained person. The problem is, however, that at facilities that do not employ nurses or highly trained medical personnel, the onus of executing complex orders like these ends up in the hands of the untrained support staff. As I mentioned, the support staff in charge of medication dispensing/observation are often unqualified, poorly trained, low-wage employees who themselves may be former addicts new to recovery. It is not unheard of for an addict to try to get a job in recovery just so they have access to medication. I had a young woman show up to an interview for a support staff position high as a kite, and when her pre-employment drug test showed positive for opioids she told me it was because of a poppy seed bagel she ate right before the interview. Right!

You may have noticed towards the top of the medication orders/taper schedule is a line that reads, "May self-administer first test dose of Suboxone 2mg SL x 1 when COWS = 13 or higher." COWS, an acronym for Clinical Opiate Withdrawal Scale, is an 11-item scale designed to determine the severity or stage of a person experiencing opioid withdrawal. What the doctor was ordering was the patient was not to start self-administering Suboxone until their COWS score was 13 or higher. The support staff were tasked with performing the COWS (CIWA in the case of an alcohol or benzodiazepine detox). While this is not a difficult task, the owners put these $12/hour support staff personnel in charge of determining when patients were ready to start taking their detox medication. I am talking about personnel whose highest levels of education were high school diplomas and who had no medical training whatsoever prior to working in a sub-acute detox environment.

If a patient who was still high on heroin started complaining they were experiencing withdrawal symptoms, and the support staff performed the COWS incorrectly and assigned the patient a higher score than what was warranted, allowing the patient to take their first test dose of Suboxone, the person would go into agonizing precipitated withdrawal. Fortunately, this never happened while I was there. But there was a situation at a nearby detox facility where a friend of mine worked in which a patient who suffered from alcohol and benzodiazepine abuse disorders was not being given their detox medications by the staff on shift because the support staff were not performing their rounds or the CIWAs correctly. The patient had to be rushed to the ER because they had a seizure. The owners of that facility, similar to mine, refused to hire nurses and instead relied upon untrained low paid labor to medically monitor and assess their patients. This is one of the reasons why patients die in treatment. Low paid, poorly trained support staff, difficult patients with underlying medical conditions, a lack of supervision and oversight, greedy unscrupulous owners, and potentially dangerous medications being administered by unqualified employees—these combine to form a volatile concoction that leads to patient fatalities.

One last item on the sample medication orders to discuss are two instructions. Notice that the doctor ordered Suboxone, Seroquel, and Klonopin. These are medications that must be separated by at least an hour due to the potential of lowering a person's blood pressure too rapidly. I cannot tell you how many times the staff did not follow these simple instructions! The other item staff had a hard time following was making sure to check the patient's blood pressure prior to administering Suboxone, Clonindine, Seroquel and Klonopin, and not to administer them if the patients' blood pressure was less than 100/60. Additional training, write ups, suspensions, and the occasional termination did little to curb repeated mistakes made by a staff, who collectively, were too unqualified to be working in a treatment setting that involved the dispensing of medication.

Most of the opioid detox patients where I worked received orders like the sample above. The doctor would start the patient out on no more than 8mg a day of Suboxone for the first two days, and would then gradually taper them off of all controlled medications over the next ten days or so. There was only one instance when the doctor increased the initial maximum daily dose of Suboxone to 16mg because the patient was not responding to the 8mg maximum. This may have been due to the fact that the patient was doing considerably more heroin than what was initially reported, or his body was just a really rapid metabolizer of Suboxone. Either way, he needed to start out on a higher initial dose of Suboxone than most.

As you can see, the patient was also tapered off of the Klonopin, which is a controlled medication (benzodiazepine), at the same time he was being tapered off of the buprenorphine. The goal in detox (or treatment) is to have a patient off of all controlled medications prior to discharge, but unfortunately, this does not always occur.

The doctor who was in charge of our patients was very experienced in the field of addiction medicine, having detoxed thousands of patients during her career. She was excellent at assessing the patients, interpreting lab results, and keeping patients comfortable without overmedicating them. Our patients were very lucky to have her. The same cannot be said about the medical director of our sister treatment facility some 200 miles away. Their doctor would routinely overmedicate the patients. Opioid detox patients were typically starting out on 30mg of Suboxone, regardless of how much dope they had been using prior to admission, and their tapers were much longer with steeper drops in dosages. The patients therefore spent a greater percentage of their treatment stay on controlled medications, and they routinely had difficulty tapering completely off of buprenorphine. Many left treatment while still on controlled medication. The doctor had very little experience working in residential treatment and facilitating patient detox, which manifested in the extent to which his patients were routinely overmedicated and would respond poorly to their therapeutic treatment. This was evidenced in the high relapse rates at our sister facility.

The takeaways

Medication is becoming more and more prevalent today in the field of addiction treatment. To capitalize on the growing number of opioid addicts seeking treatment, most treatment centers are now offering Medication Assisted Treatment (MAT), which combines pharmaceutical medications with behavioral therapy.

As intelligent as that may seem, my view is that using pharmaceutical drugs as a primary offensive tool is a dangerous slippery slope for any health concern, let alone in cases of addiction where the addicts desire to be in a constant state of euphoria. Being overmedicated on buprenorphine and benzodiazepines negates the whole point of working towards a state of sobriety. Being overmedicated in treatment renders any potential positive effects of behavioral therapy null and void. Ironically, detox and treatment centers can and do garner reputations for overprescribing medications, which actually attracts addicts looking to capitalize on having a free roof over their head, free food, and plenty of free feel-good pharmaceutical medications. Some doctors overprescribe freely to keep patient's happy as a way to entice them to stay in treatment longer while the owners continue to bill their insurance companies.

It is crucial to have a clear understanding of the medication protocols employed by the facility prior to admitting. Key questions to ask are:

- who are the doctors in charge of the medical care;
- what is their professional history (suspensions, license revocations, admonishments, etc.);
- how much experience do they have working in treatment, detox, or with drug addiction;
- are they board-certified addiction specialists;
- are patients tapered off of all controlled and non-controlled medications prior to discharge;
- if my health insurance were to lapse or if I am denied benefits while I am in your treatment facility, what happens (will you keep me until I am detoxed off of my meds or will you discharge me on medication);
- can you provide me with an example of medication orders and a taper schedule;
- what types of drugs do you normally prescribe and in what dosages during detox;

- who is in charge of dispensing the medication and what is their experience (is it support staff or a board-certified nurse);
- in the case of residential treatment, do physicians and psychiatrists work together on cases and read each other's treatment notes to make sure they are on the same page with the medications each are prescribing?

This last point is an interesting one, and comes from a personal experience I had as a sober living owner. There was a treatment center in Malibu that would send me many of their patients. When these clients would admit to my facility, my staff and I would inventory their medications, which were numerous. On a number of separate occasions, we noticed that the medical doctor and the psychiatrist would be prescribing the same medication in the same dosage for different indications. It was evident the medical staff was not communicating with one another nor were they reading the patient's charts because if they had, they would have seen they were doubling up their patient's medications.

It is very important prior to entering treatment to have a clear understanding of what the facility's physician philosophy is for treating substance abuse disorders. Do they use medication for detox and taper purposes only? Do they discharge patients on controlled medications such as Suboxone and Subutex? Do they assess each case individually or do all patients receive the same standing orders?

As mentioned, buprenorphine is extremely difficult to get off of on your own, so if you are discharged on it, there is a good chance you will be on it for the foreseeable future. If you are looking for temporary relief and to assuage your symptoms through pharmaceutical drug substitution, and you are okay with the very real possibility of being on medication for the rest of your life including daily dosing and routine physician visits, then by all means go for it. But if you do not want to be tethered to a drug or physician visits and you would prefer to transmute the addicted state of consciousness so the drive to use is no longer in your awareness, then make sure you attend a facility or see a doctor who will assist you to achieve that goal. It is imperative to have a clear intention, prior to entering rehab, of what you would like your life to look like post-treatment. Knowing this will help you choose the facility, physicians, and clinical staff who will best help you to achieve your desired outcome.

#4 - You Don't Need to Travel Across Country for Rehab

Tens of thousands of individuals per year criss cross the country to go to rehab. The lure of warm weather, ocean views, and the false promise of effective treatment entice the unsuspecting to leave home and seek healing in a new environment, one that differs from where they will eventually need to return to. Their travel is often driven by a myth that treatment is better in California or Florida than in other parts of the country. This is just not true.

While there may be treatment centers in those two states that claim to have high success rates, or that say they offer the most effective treatment available, there isn't a single treatment center in America that can factually prove the treatment it offers works for the majority of their patients. So why then do people still leave their home state, travel all the way across the country to attend a treatment center that cannot prove it is any better than the free 12-step meeting in their local church basement?

The answer is that society has been conditioned to believe residential drug rehab is an effective form of treatment when, in reality, there isn't a single shred of systematic or peer-reviewed data to support this assumption. When addicted individuals get to the point of total desperation, rehab can be an answer for some, but the numbers show it only works for roughly 5% to 10% of all those who attend 12-step treatment facilities, and there is no hard data which supports the efficacy of non-12-step treatment programs. Unfortunately, addiction in all its forms has become so prevalent today, it has led to an explosion of new treatment options all across the U.S. Wading through all of their misinformation to find a viable treatment option has become an insurmountable task for the layperson who does not understand what addiction is or what addiction treatment should be.

When people seek treatment, either they or their loved one is in a place of total desperation. But given that most people are conditioned to desire quick and easy solutions to their problems, they become susceptible to TV advertisements, fancy websites, and the salesman's hard sell. They want to BELIEVE there is an answer to be found, an answer somewhere outside of themselves in the form of a pill and some counselor's gentle spoken words.

There are some areas of the country where no treatment centers are available in-state, so going out of state is their only option. But in many cases, a patient or their loved ones are persuaded by a rehab salesman or a body broker to attend a facility far away. They don't realize the degree to which the salesman has a financial incentive to lure them in, nor do they suspect the amount of marketing hype that went into the information and pictures on the treatment center's website to make it look promising.

I am not here to judge anyone's decision making, but I do want to convey this fact: if you end up believing treatment will be more effective just because it is in California, Florida, or a state other than the one you reside in, you are setting yourself up for failure.

As I have said, not all treatment centers are the same, but the structure of most rehab treatment is virtually identical no matter where you go. This is due to the fact that the entire treatment industry is under the control of the insurance industry, a phenomenon known as managed care. The forms and methods of treatment offered today are dictated by "the minimum standards of care" required by health insurance reimbursement guidelines. Treatment centers work to satisfy these minimum standards in order to capture reimbursement.

What that means for patients is no matter where you go, you will receive some combination of medication, therapy (mostly group), some chemical dependency counseling, maybe an individual therapy session or two with a psychotherapist, and a whole lot of unnecessary urine testing. Some of the exclusive treatment centers may offer more individual therapy than group, but even they cannot prove their methods of treatment are any more effective than less expensive facilities.

Of course, not all treatment centers offer the exact same clinical programming, nor do they all subscribe to the same definition of addiction or the same treatment philosophy. There are facilities that advertise advanced brain therapies (from neurofeedback to targeted amino acid therapy which can take anywhere from 3 to 18mos to fully realize its effects), cutting edge "evidence-based" talk therapies, individualized treatment programs, and unique treatment philosophies not commonly utilized in other treatment centers. Such differences are like any business looking to differentiate themselves from their competitors. These are little more than points of marketing differentiation intended to persuade you to choose their facility over another. Overall, the basic format of all rehab treatment is virtually identical from one facility to the next.

What counts is how successful the facility is. Whatever rehab you are considering based on liking what you have read or heard, you must ask the facility to provide you with proof their program has worked. Have them identify which specific therapies they provide played a role in their patients' decision to start down the path of sobriety. I may be going out on a limb here to say few will be able to provide you with actual proof. If they do offer some form of hard evidence, such as a survey they performed, ask if it has been systematically or peer reviewed. Then please get a copy of it and send it to me, and I will help you understand it. You can email me at: info@thepowerofchoice.com.

The reason for this is that statistics can be bent to look better than they really are. It starts with the fact that treatment centers that publish success rate figures have to rely upon the self-reporting of their former clients to honestly disclose if they are still sober or back to using again. What typically happens is an employee from the facility will be tasked with calling former clients at different time intervals post-treatment to ask if they are still sober. I cannot tell you how many friends of mine from my recovery days, as well as others who have been through treatment whom I have met who have told me they falsely reported being sober when they received their checkup calls. There is an embedded shame component associated with relapse, so naturally they aren't going to tell the truth. Of course, the truth also doesn't matter to the treatment center because they can report the client is still sober, which makes their statistics look good. Consider also that for every client they get in touch with, there are scores they never reach, and given the proclivity of addicts to relapse, you can bet the individuals they cannot contact are back to using again. They don't count these clients as relapses, which in turn artificially inflates their success rate.

Here's an example. Say a facility has treated 100 clients since their inception. The aftercare director calls all 100 former clients but only manages to speak with 50, while the other 50 do not reply to the messages left. The sample size is now 50 clients, and out of those 50, let's say 25 self-report they are sober and working their program, and 25 admit to relapsing. The aftercare director can now report to the owner or CEO a 50% success rate. I have witnessed this firsthand, where the facility will tell potential clients that they have a 50% (or greater) rate of sober clients after one year, when in fact the true statistic is really 25 out of 100, e.g., a 25% success rate. While this is still above the industry average of 5% to 10% for 12-step treatment programs, you have been misled into thinking the facility is among the most successful anywhere.

It is imperative if you are looking to go to a treatment center that posts a success rate to ask for the empirical data to see how they calculated their figures. Make sure also to ask this key question: of the clients who self-reported being sober, what were the substances those patients were seeking treatment for? You need to compare success rates for the substances you or your loved one is using. For example, opioid addicts have a much higher relapse rate than other drugs of choice. So if you are seeking help for opioid addiction, you want to know what percentage of their opioid addicted patients have remained sober for at least a year following treatment. If they are unwilling to furnish you with the specific data, chances are it's because they know their numbers will not hold up under close examination. I believe this to be the primary reason why no treatment center has undertaken or can produce a systematic or peer reviewed study to support positive longitudinal success rate figures.

There was a time when traveling out of state to seek treatment was almost a requirement for many people, as there were fewer treatment options than today. But now, as the country grapples with an enormous opioid epidemic, there are shortages of beds in certain parts of the country, primarily along the East Coast. For individuals seeking help who reside in those areas, traveling out-of-state might therefore be necessary. Nevertheless, even in those cases, do your due diligence prior to admitting. Ask the questions I have provided in the preceding chapters. Speak with the owners, and members of the clinical and medical staff. Get answers and promises in writing. And if possible, try to tour the facilities you are contemplating beforehand.

A major reason to stay local

One additional point. In my view, the most important reason NOT to seek treatment away from home is that it is self-defeating. The patient is learning to create a sober life for themselves in an environment that does not mirror the one they will return to (if they are planning to return home following treatment). If you live in Connecticut and travel to southern California for treatment, so much is not the same between the two states. The environment, available aftercare resources, relapse triggers, culture, and lifestyle are fundamentally different. I cannot tell you how many times I have witnessed an individual travel from outside California where I live to attend treatment, then do well in treatment and aftercare, only to return home and relapse within days. The home environment is highly triggering. Getting together with friends you formerly used drugs or alcohol with, or going to the same locations you used in can trigger deeply engrained patterns and habits that have been cemented into both the conscious and subconscious mind. You are reminded constantly of your old rituals of scoring drugs. Simply sitting on the same couch where you used to get high can trigger the desire to use again.

When the addict learns to abstain from drugs and/or alcohol in a new environment, the triggers associated with their home-using environment remain unaddressed. This is a dangerous proposition if the person plans on returning home following treatment, where all of their old unhealthy patterns will resurface if they are not adequately prepared mentally, emotionally, physically and spiritually throughout the treatment process. Chances are, they will succumb to the siren call of their drug(s) of choice.

It is understandable to want a fresh start in life coming out the other side of rehab, and I recommend it. Whatever lifestyle choices the addict was making prior to treatment were obviously part of the problem, and those choices were made in an environment unsupportive of sound health and wellness. That said, however, to give yourself the best chance to create a sober life, it is imperative, at least initially, to start the process in an environment that mirrors the one you will live in.

If the idea of starting a brand new life elsewhere after treatment appeals to you, then by all means do so. Find a treatment option in the new state or city you would like to live in. Chances are the rehab facility will have a range of aftercare options in the area, and they will be able to help you to create a solid discharge plan to help you after leaving treatment. The faster new healthy lifestyle patterns can be implemented, the better.

Keep in mind that breaking the patterns of addiction is a difficult process that takes time. The process of creating sobriety truly begins once the individual leaves treatment and reenters life outside the walls of a rehab facility. But all this has to be planned and thought about from the start, before you choose to enter treatment in another city or state. As the saying goes, by failing to plan, you are planning to fail. It will pay off in spades to put together a cohesive post-treatment plan prior to entering treatment so the transition back into society will be seamless.

#5 - Effective Treatment is Not What You May Think It Is

The best way to dive into this topic is to explain what effective treatment is not. Effective treatment is not a one-size-fits-all approach, as we are each unique. We come from different upbringings, we have different belief systems, we vary in our health concerns, we desire different things in life, and we see our life purpose in different ways.

But for far too long, the rehab approach to treating addiction has been based on the assembly line, largely because it is an effective business model. Patients enter treatment; they're assessed, diagnosed, and usually prescribed medications. Patients receive a couple of group therapy sessions each day and maybe one or two individual therapy sessions each week with a therapist who hopefully possesses the experience and expertise to guide the patient towards a path of healing their underlying drivers of their addiction. Their treatment plan, which is largely the same as every other patient at the facility, is typically supplemented with 12-step meetings, despite having been proven to be an ineffective method of treating addiction.[16]

In the meantime, patients eat tons of refined sugar and poor-quality GMO foods which lack the nutrients required to heal the body and optimize cognitive function. They often smoke countless cigarettes or chew tobacco, drink endless caffeinated beverages, and spend a majority of their time with fellow addicts either complaining, looking to hook-up, or playing a game of one-upmanship as to who was the biggest addict while reminiscing about the glory of their using days.

This picture is what transpires at most residential treatment centers in the U.S., so it's no surprise residential treatment has proven to be an ineffective form of treating addiction. With the recent trend in Medication Assisted Treatment, we are now witnessing this same ineffective treatment married to powerful pharmaceutical medications (buprenorphine) designed to be almost impossible to get off of on your own, whose function is merely to manage the symptoms of addiction.

Ultimately, my view is that drug rehab today, as an industry, is completely failing to address the

---

[16] Marica Ferri et al, "Alcoholics Anonymous and other 12-step programmes for alcohol dependence," *The Cochrane Group*, July 19, 2006, http://www.cochrane.org/CD005032/ADDICTN_alcoholics-anonymous-aa-is-self-help-group-organised-through-an-international-organization-of-recovering-alcoholics-that-offers-emotional-support-and-a-model-of-abstinence-for-people-recovering-from-alcohol-dependence-using-a-12-step-appr

underlying drivers of the addicted consciousness. It may manage the symptoms of addiction through medication, but addiction will never be transmuted by a pill, patch, film, or any other form of pharmaceutical medication.

The bigger issue is that today, our society and the world in which we live have been designed to breed an addicted consciousness. We are addicted to money, sex, substances, control, and fame. We believe that the only path to happiness and fulfillment is through the acquisition of material goods, or perhaps through recognition. But the path to true happiness, contentment, and fulfillment can never be achieved through the ego because the only word the ego understands is MORE. More money, more sex, more drugs, more control, or more fame or recognition.

Our collective addicted consciousness is fueled by messages we see hundreds of times per day in the media. Magazines, TV, movies, newspapers, the Internet—everywhere are messages that perpetuate the notion that we should all be striving for fame and the acquisition of material goods. The problem with those goals is that they are unattainable to the masses, and they are unending. They do not intrinsically possess any form of tangible final outcome where one can say, "I finally made it." Look at how many celebrities and wealthy individuals who appear to have made it only to have their lives prematurely ended by drug addiction.

The incessant pursuit of this ego construct keeps us

on the hamster wheel of life, chasing a golden carrot that will always remain out of reach. The pursuit feeds the ego, but never satisfies it. It has become worse in today's world, as social media platforms reinforce the messaging as our peers routinely celebrate themselves and their most recent acquisition or experience. Social media encourages people to be constantly looking for validation as to how important they are or how great their life looks like through the lens or perceptions of their friends and followers.

The current social paradigm we live in perpetuates this endless cycle of desire, which is followed by various degrees of suffering. For many, the respite of choice from their failure to achieve happiness is through substances. Some end up seeking solace in a liquor store or a bar. Others through a prescription pad or a dealer on the street. Any way it's done, we all make our own choices as to how we alleviate the inevitable suffering that accompanies the journey of life, to which there are tangible consequences for choosing poorly.

To truly cure addiction, we must first learn to shift our consciousness from the lower nature (ego) to our higher nature. To do that, we must recognize the presence of this ego, how it manifests through our thoughts, words, and deeds, and then work diligently to overcome its vice grip on our soul. This process cannot, and will not happen in a 30, 60, or 90-day residential or outpatient rehab program whose healing programs and preferred methodologies are dictated by the narrow constraints of our current managed care healthcare system. The goal of substituting one drug for another under the argument that lives are saved because addicts are not overdosing is not a solution. We cannot simply seek to manage cravings with "legal" forms of pharmaceutical opioids or other medications designed to reduce cravings. Pharmaceutical medication does always diminish the criminality associated with the addict lifestyle simply because addicts can see doctor dealers for their scripts instead of street dealers.

If you accept the simple version of rehab, then the current model that the rehab industry employs may be for you. But if you will accept my advice and become one of those who would truly like to transmute the physical and psychological hooks of addiction and an addicted consciousness, then here is what effective treatment for addiction in all of its forms looks like.

What truly effective treatment is

To begin, the process of healing from addiction begins with you, as a unique individual. It requires a careful, deep, and thorough assessment of your personal history as to how and why you (or your loved one) became addicted to your drug(s) or processes of choice. The physiological drivers of addiction need to be handled either through pharmaceutical medication (temporarily), plant medicine (Ayahuasca and/or

Ibogaine), supplements, organic plant based foods, or a combination of the aforementioned. The body needs to detox and rid itself of as many foreign chemicals as possible as their effects on emotional regulation and cognition do impair one's consciousness.

Effective treatment also means uncovering and understanding the emotional drivers of addiction. As I previously mentioned, a major problem with the current pharmaceutical method of detox and symptom management is that many of the drugs used in a rehab setting interfere with a person's ability to access their emotions. Emotional dysregulation is a primary driver of addiction, and learning to feel one's emotions and to work with them in a healthy fashion are thus primary elements in transmuting addiction.

Effective treatment also requires, in my view, a little bit of suffering, both physical and financial. The problem with pharmaceutical detox is that it alleviates physical suffering almost too well. You may be asking yourself: Why suffer? Why not take detox drugs? Why would anyone want to experience the suffering associated with detox? Perhaps my answer sounds like "tough love," but it is because patients will respect their sobriety to a greater degree if they truly feel their detox. There is wisdom to be gained through the process of suffering, and for some, the memory of a hard detox can be the difference maker when those newly in recovery are tempted to start using again after they leave treatment. People often fail to respect what comes easily to them when it does not require sacrifice and effort.

As for financial suffering, health insurance for rehab has been detrimental to its effectiveness. For many, it is simply too easy to access treatment. A $500 insurance premium and the waiving of co-pays does not require the addict to have enough "skin in the game" regarding treatment. If a patient could not rely upon insurance benefits, or a friend or loved one to pay for their treatment and they were personally responsible to pay, say a minimum of $10,000 every time they went through treatment, they might respect the process more. They may feel compelled to make more of an effort to lead a sober life post-treatment. As it stands now, the revolving door of treatment will continue to go around and around due to this combination of poor medical and therapeutic intervention, and a lack of personal investment and sacrifice in the name of sobriety on behalf of the addict.

The final element in effective rehab is to take a holistic approach. Once the body has been rid of the chemicals that interfere with cognitive function, emotional regulation, and physiological function, the process of reconciling with the underlying drivers of addiction must commence. It is imperative that rehab address the mental, emotional, physical and spiritual aspects of the Self equally. One should have a treatment team comprised of individuals who are adept at healing these four facets of one's being.

My concierge treatment service

It is challenging to provide an example of what holistic treatment looks like because most people think of rehab that is facilitated in a hospital and residential setting. But let me describe what I have learned to provide after my decade in the industry. I work with my clients in what I call a concierge treatment program, meaning it is completely customized to each individual's needs in an environment that closely mirrors the one they will be returning to. Clients who come to me are first medically assessed and stabilized. I order comprehensive blood labs to check a myriad of potential underlying health conditions that can contribute to the desire to self-medicate, including testing neurotransmitter function. Once the detoxification process starts, I then begin to implement a wide-ranging, holistic treatment plan.

My clients begin with a combination of energy medicine and esoteric acupuncture to activate and align their chakras and higher heart. Whether or not you believe in these modalities, they open the gateway to a path of healing. They also go through sessions of talk therapy, facilitated by seasoned therapists who possess no less than 20 years' experience working with addiction and acute mental health concerns. The clients also start receiving personal physical training to strengthen the body. This is supplemented by therapeutic yoga, breath work, and meditation. No two client programs are ever the same, nor are their durations.

A curious phenomenon associated with addiction is the condition of disembodiment. In its simplest definition, disembodiment is the state where an individual is in their body, but the body and mind are on autopilot; it's an unconscious reactive condition. When we introduce powerful substances like drugs and alcohol, they have the tendency to hijack our true Self, and this autopilot condition takes over. Therapeutic yoga, breath work, and meditation are powerful tools used as a means to reintegrate clients with their Mind/Body to reinitiate *conscious* living. Some additional supplemental modalities include high-performance neuro-feedback, Qi Gong, Tai-Chi, nutritional counseling, and other treatment or therapies I believe invaluable to improving the client's condition.

Trauma is the new buzz word in treatment, and many therapists in the field believe addiction is rooted in the trauma one experiences within their life. While there may be truth to the speculation, no direct scientific correlation has been shown. However, I have all of my clients work with a clinician who specializes in Somatic Experiencing, which seeks to address residual conscious and subconscious trauma conditions that may be impairing their sense of happiness and inner peace. Somatic Experiencing is a therapeutic technique developed by Dr. Peter Levine. I have found it to be a powerful tool to help individuals overcome residual trauma that remains in their conscious or unconscious and which may be an underlying driver of addict behavior. If you are an addicted person who suffers from a traumatic experience, make sure there are qualified trauma specialists on staff at the facility you plan to attend. I would highly recommend finding a facility that specifically employs Somatic Experiencing practitioners. Art therapy can also be a powerful medium to work with residual trauma, but it is rare to find qualified art therapists on staff at residential or hospital treatment facilities.

My philosophy also teaches clients to look at food not as a source of enjoyment, but rather as a source of fuel and medicine. We teach our clients to ask themselves: What is the best source of fuel to put into my body," and then to listen to what their body tells them. Your body is like a car—if you put higher quality fuel in the tank, it will operate better. But if you put cheap gas in the engine, the car will sputter and eventually break down, leaving you stranded on the side of the road (relapse).

Refined sugar and GMO foods should be avoided at all costs. The brain needs to repair itself to heal from addiction, but when refined sugar is consumed, the same neurotransmitters in the brain that get activated with drugs and alcohol are stimulated. The brain does not have the ability to differentiate between sugar and drugs, so while parts of the body are detoxifying from the drugs or alcohol, the brain is not able to repair itself. Opioid and alcohol addicts often crave sugar while they are detoxing or going through treatment because their brains are craving stimulation. It is imperative that if you or your loved one is exploring treatment to overcome addiction that you completely abstain from refined sugar to allow your brain to repair itself. The same goes for avoiding cigarettes and caffeine.

We also initiate the process of teaching our clients how to free themselves from attachment. Attachment to our visual appearance, attachment to money and material possessions, attachment to substances, attachment to euphoria, attachment to the need for validation, attachment to others, attachment in any form feeds the ego, which can only result in a state of perpetual suffering. The most common way for addicts to temporarily assuage the discomfort associated with their suffering is by resorting to using drugs, alcohol, promiscuous sex and technology as coping mechanisms. We teach our clients to be aware of the causes of suffering, and we prepare them to deal with the inevitable discomfort associated with a four-letter word call L-I-F-E.

As I've reviewed, one of the biggest shortcomings of residential and hospital treatment today is the environment. Anyone can become abstinent in the artificial surroundings of these settings, but one of the leading causes of relapse is succumbing to the triggers addicts face once they return home. It is thus imperative to learn how to create sobriety in an environment that mirrors the one you will be returning to. Our clients stay in either a condo or a house by themselves while accompanied by a sober companion. Sober companionship is a vital component to our approach because the demonstration of addictive behavior or consciousness more often than not will appear outside of a therapy session in the form of a spoken word or deed. Our sober companions are essentially life coaches whose secondary function is to point out these behaviors as they present, bringing awareness to the client of what their unconscious behaviors are as they happen, and work with them to transmute these ego manifestations in the moments they occur. As a tertiary function, they accompany our clients home post-treatment during their first few weeks or months to serve as a safeguard against them succumbing to any triggers they may experience in their home environment.

All of the treatments our clients receive are either facilitated in the residence, or offices of the clinicians they are working with. Our clients engage in anywhere from 30 to over 40 hours a week of individual treatment. During their downtime, they will spend time out in the community accompanied by their companions doing normal things and just enjoying them for what they are – going out to dinner, movies, walking, dancing, hiking, spending time in nature at a park, beach or in the mountains, and engaging in routine activities they can continue at home. Breaking the cycle of addiction requires not only healing the underlying mental, emotional, spiritual and physiological drivers of addiction. It is also about creating new patterns of living, learning to engage in healthy fun activities that satisfy the soul. The void of no longer using drugs and alcohol needs to be filled with activities that support a foundation on which a sober life can be built.

One point I make to all of my clients is to look at life as if it were a wheel; at the center hub of the wheel is You. Each spoke in the wheel is a facet of one's life that comprises who you are, and what makes you, You. The spokes can represent friends, family, hobbies, work, relationships, passion projects, spiritual pursuits, fitness, physical and mental health, etc. Those addicted to drugs and alcohol typically have a highly unbalanced wheel, with one spoke overloaded because the addict is only concerned with that facet – this is the spoke of getting high. Lasting sobriety is created by removing the getting-high spoke, focusing instead on creating or reestablishing connections with other healthy spokes, in equal parts, to create a well-rounded wheel. We do not focus on abstinence or sobriety per se. Rather, we focus on teaching clients to pay attention to and build their healthy spokes, creating balance. We help them understand what to do if they begin feeling overloaded in any particular area. Creating a sober life is easier when the goal is not focusing on the sobriety itself, but instead focusing on making healthy self-supportive choices that strengthen existing healthy spokes or to create new spokes in the wheel upon which a healthy and happy life can be fashioned.

We don't view ourselves as rehab owners or counselors, but as healers and teachers who show our clients how to facilitate change within their lives. We seek to disseminate information and wisdom gained through our own studies and life experiences. We teach independence, conscious "mindful" healthy living, and the power associated with one's free will. In general, our approach is opposite most residential treatment or 12-step groups which promote co-dependent relationships. We want our clients to thrive and spread their wings when they re-enter their lives. We don't want repeat clients.

An in-home alternative

If neither the residential or hospital treatment works for you, nor the concierge approach I use, there are other options. For instance, you even have the ability to create your own treatment program from the comfort of your home if you so choose. If you have health insurance or financial means, you can seek out a physician who can create an in-home medical detox program. I would recommend having someone handle the medication to limit the potential for abuse. Also, find a physician who can test and rebalance your neurotransmitter function. Beyond that, you can find healers, teachers or clinicians who can teach you how to heal yourself, to tap into your intrinsic gifts, are willing to share their insights without ulterior motive, and who can show you how to maximize your potential. There are many qualified behavioral therapists and clinicians who take insurance.

But also, go find a yoga studio close by and begin a yoga practice. Research healthy organic plant-based diets, change your eating habits, and detoxify your body by using food as medicine. 95% of the body's serotonin is found in the gut so it is imperative to remove the parasites caused by GMO's and meat, and begin to put nutrient-rich, high-quality plant-based foods in your system. [17] Go to the gym and work out three to four times a week. Find a spiritual outlet or begin a spiritual practice of any kind that resonates with you and your beliefs. The process of spiritual development or establishing a strong spiritual connection with a god of your belief or a universal Source fosters humility and gratitude, two foundational traits that are vital to achieving a sense of peace, happiness, and overall well-roundedness.

---

[17] Adam Hadhazy, "Think Twice: How the Gut's "Second Brain" Influences Mood and Well Being." *Scientific American*, February 12, 2010, https://www.scientificamerican.com/article/gut-second-brain/

In the early stages of recovery, it is imperative to treat the process like a 40-hour a week job, and do not quit no matter how hard it gets. By not succumbing to triggers, and through perseverance, you will create little victories for yourself, which over time add up to huge wins! With each successive healthy choice, you create momentum that will propel you forward with tremendous speed. The temptation to succumb to triggers will diminish, I promise!

Patience, perseverance and promises

The "one-size-fits-all" residential approach to treating addiction does not work for the majority of addicts, though it remains the standard model of rehab some 60 years after the first residential treatment center in the U.S. was created. But there are now other modalities to choose from, as I have presented. Everyone's healing path is different, and what might work for some may not work for others. Treating addiction is no different.

Whatever process you select, know that true healing is a fluid, multi-faceted progression that is long in duration. In fact, it never truly ends, just as all life is a journey. As you open new doors along the path, you will be continually confronted with interesting new beginnings. The recovery process is not an easy one, but it is rewarding. Many will stumble along the way, and that is okay. The key is to pay attention to and learn from what works for you and what doesn't, and then to try to keep using the tactics that work. Do not be critical of yourself if you fall down. If you stumble, try not to stay down. Pick yourself back up, dust yourself off, and keep moving forward. The simple counting of sober days is not what is important. It is the personal wisdom gained during the journey that ultimately matters most, as that knowledge will assist you to stay on the path to creating a life filled with health and happiness.

I believe that realignment with your Soul's purpose is the key component to transmuting addiction. Seek to discover your true life's purpose, and work ceaselessly to achieve realistic short-term, medium-term, and long-term goals towards it. Remove as many chemicals from your life as you can by going green. Eat clean, organic plant based non-GMO food. Exercise your mind, body, and spirit every day in equal parts. Learn to meditate. As best as possible, stay away from social media and turn off your television, smart phone, tablet and computer (all highly addicting and are a medium for mind control). Instead, read books and take classes that interest you. Stop paying attention to the opinions of others, learn to listen to your intuition for it will always steer you in the right direction, and start paying attention to the signs and symbols the Universe puts in your path that are intended to help guide you in the right direction.

Know that you alone have the power to create the life you ultimately envision for yourself—all it takes is a little perseverance in the face of adversity. Do not buy into the false belief that the purpose of life is to acquire as much money, fame, and as many material possessions as possible. This is an illusion intended to enslave the minds of the masses, and it is a life path that only leads to suffering. The goal of life is to be happy, and happiness can be achieved by practicing gratitude, living clean, and aligning with your Soul's true purpose. Learn how to give and receive unconditional love, which in the early stages of recovery requires work. Loving yourself and others is a choice one must make, and that choice is yours and yours alone.

Blessings...

> If you are interested in finding out more about The Power of Choice™, Concierge Addiction Treatment, or our Holistic Retreats, please contact us through our web site at:
> http://www.thepowerofchoice.com/contact-us-1/
>   &
> Keep an eye out for my forthcoming book:
> "The Fraudulent World of Drug Rehab & Why It Doesn't Work"

www.ingramcontent.com/pod-product-compliance
Lightning Source LLC
Chambersburg PA
CBHW031554040426
42452CB00006B/304